The Trials of Ezra Pound

Other plays by Timothy Findley

The Stillborn Lover
Can You See Me Yet?

THE TRIALS OF
EZRA POUND

BY TIMOTHY FINDLEY

Blizzard Publishing • Winnipeg

The Trials of Ezra Pound first published 1994 by
Blizzard Publishing Inc.
73 Furby Street, Winnipeg, Canada R3C 2A2
© 1995 Pebble Productions Inc.

Cover art by Robert Pasternak.
Printed in Canada by Friesen Printers.

Published with the assistance of
the Canada Council and the Manitoba Arts Council.

Canadian Cataloguing in Publication Data

Findley, Timothy, 1930–
The trials of Ezra Pound
    A play.
    ISBN 0-921368-50-X
    1. Pound, Ezra, 1885–1972—Drama.
I. Title.
PS8511.I38T7 1995   C812'.54   C95-920038-X
PR9199.3.F53T7 1995

The Trials of Ezra Pound was first presented in 1990 as a radio play by the Canadian Broadcasting Corporation, produced by Damiano Pietropaolo and starring Douglas Rain as Ezra Pound.

Preface

This play is based, in part, on transcripts of the preliminary hearings held in Washington, D.C., in late 1945 and early 1946. Their purpose was to establish whether or not Ezra Pound was mentally fit to stand trial for treason—charges based on the fascist propaganda he broadcast from Italy during World War II. In the course of the hearings, Ezra Pound spoke only once, saying: "I never did believe in Fascism." *The Trials of Ezra Pound* is an exploration of what he did not say at this hearing. The passages spoken by Pound when broadcasting are taken from transcripts of his actual words.

The historical facts are these: Ezra Pound was found unfit to stand trial and was committed to St. Elizabeth's Hospital in Washington, D.C., where he remained from 1946 to 1958. Released on the condition that he live out his days in Italy, Pound returned there to take up residence in Rapallo with his mistress, Olga Rudge. In 1972, he died—as he had predicted—in Venice, where he is buried on the island of San Michele.

7

Characters

EZRA: Ezra Pound, the American poet. He is sixty years old.

WILLIAMS: William Carlos Williams, the American poet and pediatrician—a longtime friend of Pound. He is sixty-three.

MUNCIE: Dr. Wendell Muncie, consulting psychiatrist, Gallinger's Hospital, Washington, D.C.

OVERHOLSER: Dr. Winfred Overholser, Superintendent of St. Elizabeth's Hospital, Washington, D.C.

JUDGE: Chief Justice Bolitha Laws, a Southerner with "courtly" manners.

CORNELL: Julien Cornell, Defense Attorney.

MATLACK: Isaiah Matlack, Assistant Attorney General of the United States.

ANDERSON: Donald Anderson, Department of Justice.

DEUTSCH: Albert Deutsch, reporter.

BEATTY: Arthur Beatty, a custodian at Gallinger's Hospital.

DALMAU: Dr. Carlos Dalmau, St. Elizabeth's Hospital, Washington, D.C.

FOREMAN: Juror March, male, the Jury Foreman.

DOROTHY: Dorothy Shakespeare, Ezra's English wife, in her early sixties.

MARTINELLI: Sheri Martinelli, a young American artist, briefly Pound's mistress and protégé.

CLERK: The court clerk, male.

RECORDER: Miss Adams, the court recorder.

REPORTER ONE / ORDERLY ONE: Male, twenties.

BAILIFF / ORDERLY TWO: Male, thirties.

REPORTER TWO / FEMALE PATIENT: Female, twenties.

TOADY: An assistant to Dr. Overholser.

Additional characters may include jurors, spectators, other members of the Press.

The Set

The basic setting is a courtroom in Washington, D.C., circa 1946. Such courts are not darkly panelled; the feeling is that of a traditional early American Meeting House, painted white with tall, multi-paned windows. The stage contains four levels: down stage is the floor of the stage itself; midway up stage a platform reached by wide steps along its front edges. Up stage of this is a higher platform, reached by two more wide steps. Furthest up stage is the Judge's desk, angled towards stage left. When the Judge is seated, his figure will dominate the court. A scrim, upon which various images can be thrown, curves from left to right, its top rising out of sight.

Below the Judge's desk, the platform holds two chairs stage right, one for the Court Clerk, one for the Court Recorder. They share a narrow table on which each has a microphone, plus a typing device for the Recorder. Stage left on the same platform is the witness chair. Beside this there is no table, but a microphone on a stand.

The central and deepest platform has a table and chair stage right for the Defence and, stage left, a table and two chairs for the Prosecution. Each table has the appropriate microphones. Depending on the size of the cast, the front of the jury box may be seen at the extreme right end of this platform, between the area for the Clerk and Recorder and the Defense area. Similarly, the fronts of the public and press galleries may be seen on the same platform, down stage left of the Prosecution.

On the floor level, down stage centre of the Defense, is Pound's chair and table, with a microphone. He rarely sits there, but everything said to him during the hearing is addressed to this chair, which is spotlit. Down stage left is a five-foot table on casters, which can serve as Muncie's desk; the Reporters' telephone station; a table in the restaurant where Deutsch and Williams eat, and as the urinals in the Courthouse and at Gallinger's Hospital. Centre stage, a stool and a long, low table represent Pound's room first at Gallinger's and then at St. Elizabeth's.

As the play unfolds, each acting area is lit and peopled according to Pound's interpretation of the events and confrontations taking place. The director and designer are invited to use rear projections throughout that will enhance the sense of turmoil in the mind of Ezra Pound—perhaps of historical figures (Roosevelt, Jefferson, Mussolini, T. S. Eliot, for instance)—perhaps of pertinent historical moments (Italian Black Shirts on the march, the death of Mussolini and his mistress, etc.). Elements of the set and prop items unavailable to a production can be mimed or adapted from other items already on stage.

Prelude

(The stage is in darkness, except for the back scrim, which should be lit with enough winter light to silhouette the structures and furniture of the empty courtroom. A single spotlight slowly reveals EZRA POUND, seated on a wooden stool. Silence, but for the sound of wind as it might be heard in Ezra's mind.)

EZRA: *(Voice over.)* This is not a work of fiction, nor yet of one man.

(The spotlight fades to darkness.)

Act One

Scene One

(Lights come up down stage left: Gallinger's Hospital, Washington, D.C. MUNCIE is seated in his office. He is writing. As the light spreads, we see WILLIAMS—dressed for winter—standing at some distance in front of the desk. The sound of the wind fades.)

WILLIAMS: *(Before full light reaches him.)* Doctor Muncie? Doctor Muncie? *(Steps into full light.)* William Carlos Williams. Pardon my mitts ...

(WILLIAMS crosses to the desk. MUNCIE rises. They shake hands.)

MUNCIE: You are late, Doctor Williams.

WILLIAMS: The train. Yes. The snow.

MUNCIE: I see.

WILLIAMS: Is Mister Pound ... expecting me?

MUNCIE: No. I'm trying to determine the state of his memory. I'm eager to see if he'll know who you are without prompting.

WILLIAMS: *(With good humour.)* He may not want to recognize me, Doctor Muncie. Ezra Pound and I don't always get along, you know.

MUNCIE: It wouldn't surprise me. At this stage, Mister Pound doesn't appear to get along with anyone. *(Moves forward.)* Would you come with me?

(MUNCIE leading, they start across the front of the stage toward stage right.)

You've known one another for several years, I understand.

WILLIAMS: Since our college days. Yes. Penn University. Nineteen-oh-two—forty-three years ago—and feels like it.

(They stop. MUNCIE mimes pressing an elevator button. They wait.)

MUNCIE: Are you in medicine, Doctor Williams? That wasn't clear in our telephone conversation. I know, of course, that you and Mister Pound are fellow poets. Here we are.

(They enter the elevator, and turn to face front. MUNCIE presses the button to start its rise.)

WILLIAMS: I'm in pediatrics, Doctor Muncie. The "poetry" of childhood.

MUNCIE: Children's poetry. I had no idea.

WILLIAMS: No. Not children's poetry, Doctor. Heavens! *(Laughs.)* I'm a pediatrician who writes poetry. For adults.

MUNCIE: I see. *(Pause.)* This way.

(They leave the elevator and start walking towards stage left.)

WILLIAMS: Is this a psychiatric hospital?

MUNCIE: No. A general hospital. This is our psychiatric wing.

(WILLIAMS stops. MUNCIE looks back.)

WILLIAMS: Is Ezra Pound dangerous?

MUNCIE: Are you afraid of him?

WILLIAMS: Not in the least. It's just that Mister Pound and I have waged many wars in the past. He may want to throw his shoes at me.

MUNCIE: He doesn't wear shoes. Only bed socks.

(MUNCIE starts away again, stopping near EZRA's centre stage area. WILLIAMS follows, and also stops.)

This is it. Are you ready?

(WILLIAMS nods and follows MUNCIE "through the door." As the lights rise, EZRA is seen lying on the low table—his "cot"—his back to the audience.)

Scene Two

MUNCIE: Mister Pound. You have a visitor.

EZRA: *(Slowly rolling over. He has almost lost his voice.)* Bill Williams?

WILLIAMS: Hello, Ezrie.

EZRA: *(Sitting up. He revels in eccentric voices, and now deliberately*

exaggerates a New Jersey accent.) Wal, now. If it ain't the Bard of
Rutherford, New Jersey. What brings you here to hell?

WILLIAMS: You.

EZRA: Me, eh? Wal—I been here some time, now. Flossie with you?

WILLIAMS: No. But she sends her love.

EZRA: That person with you—who might that be?

MUNCIE: Doctor Muncie, Mister Pound.

EZRA: Never heard of him. *(Pause. He reverts to his own voice, half
whispering.)* They're trying to make me say I'm crazy, Bill. Stand up
in public and say I'm crazy—otherwise they'll hang me. That man
there's the hangman. Goes by the name of Muncie—calls himself a
doctor. But I know better.

WILLIAMS: Unh-hunh ...

EZRA: I'm drowning here, Bill. Drowning.

WILLIAMS: You look dry enough to me.

EZRA: No, no. I'm drowning. Drowning. *(Pause.)* You remember that
dog we saved. When we were kids? That dog?

WILLIAMS: No, Ez. I don't.

EZRA: Yes, you do. Swimming. Kids. We'd gone for a swim in the river
by Wyncote, north of Philadelphia. Summer of—I don't remember—
eighteen-ninety ... something—you and me and that dog. There was
a sudden storm. The rain came rushing down—and the river swelled.
And this dog ...

WILLIAMS: I don't remember.

EZRA: He was a terrier. Terrier with pale front paws that beat against the
water ...

WILLIAMS: No. I—

EZRA: Head up—eyes gone red with terror. A small, brown dog and you
and me went out—swam out and saved it.

WILLIAMS: No. I never did that, Ezra. Must have been you and someone else.

EZRA: You goddamned liar. You know damn well it was you. Liar.
Liar! (He quietens.) This is me, Bill. Me, here. Drowning. *(Suddenly.)*
Help me! Help!

MUNCIE: Doctor Williams—I guess you'd better leave.

EZRA: Help me. *Help!*

WILLIAMS: No. I'd rather—

EZRA: Help me! Aiuto! Help!

(MUNCIE starts to escort WILLIAMS off towards the right.)

MUNCIE: Thank you for coming ...

(They exit.)

EZRA: *Help! Help! Help! Help! Help!*

Scene Three

(Courtroom. EZRA's cries are suddenly stopped by the sound of a gavel. This is the signal for lights to come up on the JUDGE, the CLERK and the chair supposed to be occupied by EZRA during the hearing. The lights have a component of strong colour. The JUDGE bangs his gavel a second time.)

CLERK: *(Rising.)* The case of Ezra Pound.

JUDGE: Swear the jury.

CLERK: *(Facing off right.)* The jurors will stand and raise your right hands.

EZRA: *(Seated centre stage, "broadcasting" in a brisk, paternal, mock folksy tone.)* Europe calling: Ezra Pound speaking ...

JUDGE: *(Looking off right.)* The case which the jury will be impanelled to hear is one involving Ezra Pound ...

EZRA: *(Still "broadcasting.")* Had you had the sense to eliminate Roosevelt and his Jews—or the Jews and their Roosevelt—at the last election, you would not now be at war. For the United States to be making war on Italy and on Europe is just plain nonsense.

JUDGE: *(Indicating the empty chair.)* Mister Pound is seated here. Will you stand, Mister Pound?

EZRA: You are not going to win this war! You never had a chance to win this war—

JUDGE: *(Bangs his gavel.)* Mister Pound—

EZRA: You know, the Jews have a law and the main purpose of this law is to provide fines payable to a gang or tribe of allegedly religious superiors—who seem—

(The JUDGE bangs his gavel.)

... who seem to have had no particular ethical status. I ask you: why was Christ crucified?

JUDGE: *(Gavel.)* Mister Pound. Will you stand?

EZRA: He was crucified for trying to bust a racket!

JUDGE: *(Gavel.)* Mister Pound, will you stand and face the prospective jurors!

Scene Four

(One final bang of the gavel is the signal for courtroom lights to snap out, and lights to snap on down stage left. The courthouse corridor. Two REPORTERS are reading their copy into telephones on the movable table. Their voices overlap.)

REPORTER ONE: For Ezra Pound, the American poet accused of treason ...

REPORTER TWO: Ezra Pound, looking pale and thin, went on trial today in a bid to establish his innocence ... yes ... that's right ... pale and thin ...

REPORTER ONE: ... this is only a preliminary trial in which his lawyers will attempt to prove that, due to insanity, the poet is unable to participate in his own defense ...

(DEUTSCH dashes out to join them.)

REPORTER TWO: Judge Bolitha Laws looked stern as he directed the selection of the jury ...

(REPORTER TWO waves at DEUTSCH and continues to talk in a lower tone into the telephone.)

REPORTER ONE: Hey, Deutsch!

DEUTSCH: Hi, Sam. Don't bother me now. I gotta get this copy in ... *(He picks up the telephone.)* Hi. Hello. This is Deutsch. Who's that? Marvin? Yeah—well. I'm at the courthouse. *Court house!*

REPORTER ONE: My line does that all the time—cuts out like that.

DEUTSCH: Sam ... Do you mind? *(He speaks into the telephone.)* Marvin? I got copy. You ready?

REPORTER ONE: So Ezra Pound is going to plead insane, eh?

DEUTSCH: You got it, Sam. Son-of-a-bitch goddamn fascist! *(Into the phone.)* Marvin? What the hell's the problem? Hurry up, will ya?

REPORTER ONE: You think he is insane?

DEUTSCH: Are you kidding? Are you kidding? Ezra Pound is about as insane as my left elbow! *(Into the phone.)* Marvin? Good ...

Scene Five

(Courthouse corridor. Through the following, lights slowly rise on the Courtroom, while the rest of the court officials, including the RECORDER and the BAILIFF, file in and take their places. EZRA lies once again on his cot, with his back to the audience.)

DEUTSCH: Here it is. Dateline: Wednesday, February 13th, 1946, Washington, D.C. Ezra Pound stands in the crowded Courtroom, surrounded by his enemies and a very few of his friends ...

(WILLIAMS enters from the right and starts walking across the down stage area, headed for the steps at the extreme left, leading to the public and press galleries.)

Pound, the American expatriate whose home has been in Italy now for almost a quarter century—and the man considered by many to be the world's greatest living poet—has been brought back to the U.S.A., accused of treason ... *(He sees WILLIAMS.)* Marvin, hang on a second. Doctor Williams! *(Into the phone.)* Look, Marvin, I'll call you back in five, okay? Keep the pencil warm ...

(WILLIAMS, having passed on by, now stops to blow his nose. DEUTSCH approaches him.)

Doctor Williams, excuse me, but before you go on in—

WILLIAMS: Not now, young man—

DEUTSCH: Please, sir. This will only take a minute and you won't miss anything in there. They haven't even chosen the jury yet.

WILLIAMS: All right—fire away. But first of all, tell me your name.

DEUTSCH: Albert Deutsch—I write for a paper called *P.M.*

WILLIAMS: How do you do?

DEUTSCH: Doctor Williams—your relation to Ezra Pound. Surely this puts you in a unique position regarding this trial.

WILLIAMS: *(Mildly amused.)* What makes you think that?

DEUTSCH: Well, William Carlos Williams is one of the best known poets in the country. People would pay attention to your opinion of Ezra Pound's poetry ...

WILLIAMS: The trouble is he's not on trial because of his poetry.

DEUTSCH: Should a poet stand trial because of things he says?

WILLIAMS: Well, he certainly shouldn't stand trial because of what he's written. But for what he's said? A poet, after all, is still a citizen.

I do know this: his broadcasts from Italy were lavishly anti-Semitic, but ... treason? *(Looks at his watch.)* I'd better get along now. I'm very anxious to sit down ...

DEUTSCH: Just one more thing, Doctor Williams. As a doctor—

WILLIAMS: I'm not a psychiatrist.

DEUTSCH: No. But as a doctor, tell me your opinion of this insanity plea. Is it justified?

WILLIAMS: That's what this trial is about, Mister Deutsch. I cannot say more until I know more.

DEUTSCH: You think Mister Pound has crazy ideas?

WILLIAMS: From time to time.

DEUTSCH: Is he possessed?

WILLIAMS: It seems so. Yes. From time to time.

DEUTSCH: Doctor Williams—

WILLIAMS: I have come to attend this hearing, Mister Deutsch. And I am going in. Now.

(WILLIAMS crosses to the steps, mounts them and disappears in the direction of the Public Gallery. DEUTSCH shrugs and returns to the telephones, where the lights fade.)

Scene Six

(Courtroom. JUDGE bangs the gavel three times. All court officials stand up. The sound startles EZRA into sitting up on his cot.)

CLERK: The United States District Court for the District of Columbia: Judge Bolitha Laws presiding.

(EZRA stands up, yawns and stretches.)

JUDGE: Certain representations have been made to the Court that Mister Pound is not in mental condition such as that he is able to participate with counsel in the trial of a criminal case ...

EZRA: Participate? I'm standing here, aren't I?

CORNELL: *(Sotto voce, to EZRA's official, but empty, chair.)* Mister Pound, I have warned you. You are to remain absolutely silent.

EZRA: *(Mimicking him while crossing to him.)* Absolutely silent?

CORNELL: *(Sotto voce.)* Yes, sir.

EZRA: *(Sotto voce.)* You got a hope in hell of that, Mister Cornell.

CORNELL: And you have a hope in hell, if you break silence one more time. I beg of you, Mister Pound.

JUDGE: Counsel.

CORNELL: Yes, Your Honor?

JUDGE: The Court has the floor at this moment.

(General laughter.)

CORNELL: Yes, Your Honor.

EZRA: The old fart.

JUDGE: *(Not hearing the remark, as most of what EZRA says is spoken only in his mind.)* I was saying: Mister Pound, according to certain representations, is not in mental condition to participate with counsel in the trial of a criminal case because he is not in a position to understand the full nature of the charges against him. Based upon that showing, which has been made to me by psychiatrists, I am going to impanel the jury to pass upon that question. You may be seated.

(EZRA remains standing where he is, until CORNELL makes a pleading gesture towards the empty chair. EZRA shrugs, and sits on his centre stage stool.)

Now appearing for Ezra Pound is Mister Julien Cornell of New York. Will you stand, please?

(Before CORNELL can move, EZRA shoots to his feet with a triumphant look over at him. EZRA will wander around the court during the following, perching on steps, staring at speakers.)

CORNELL: *(Standing.)* Your Honor.

JUDGE: Thank you, Mister Cornell. Representing the United States Government in this case is Mister Matlack ...

MATLACK: *(Rising.)* Your Honor.

JUDGE: ... and Mister Donald Anderson from the Department of Justice.

ANDERSON: Your Honor.

JUDGE: You may be seated, gentlemen.

(They sit. The JUDGE looks off right.)

Ladies and gentlemen of the jury—I must now ask if any one of you knows Ezra Pound.

BEATTY: *(Off right.)* I do.

JUDGE: What is your name?

BEATTY *(Off.)* Arthur Beatty. *(Pronounced "Batey.")*

JUDGE: Come forward, please.

(BEATTY appears right and stands facing the JUDGE.)

How long have you known Mister Pound, Mister Beatty?

BEATTY: Ever since he has been there in the hospital.

(EZRA approaches BEATTY and stares at him.)

JUDGE: You are referring to a hospital here in Washington?

BEATTY: Yes, sir. Though, of late, he seems to have disappeared. I cannot tell where Mister Pound is now ...

JUDGE: You work at Gallinger's Hospital, Mister Beatty? Where Mister Pound was lately under observation?

BEATTY: Yes, Your Honor. I'm one o' the custodians. Nights.

EZRA: You're a goddamned garbage hoister in the goddamned latrine, you pee-smelling buffoon. Say it!

JUDGE: Do you know some of the facts with reference to this matter, Mister Beatty?

BEATTY: Yes. I heard him—nights.

JUDGE: Be more specific, Mister Beatty. For the record.

EZRA: *(Walking towards the movable table, which will serve as a urinal in the next scene.)* Tell'm the contents of my bowels, Beatty. That's what he wants!

BEATTY: I'm not sure I understand the question, Your Honor.

JUDGE: You say you "heard him—nights." You mean Mister Pound?

(EZRA makes a hopeless gesture, and walks behind the movable table, undoes his fly and begins to urinate.)

BEATTY: Yessir. He talked. Sometimes till dawn.

JUDGE: To you, Mister Beatty?

(Lights begin to fade in courtroom.)

BEATTY: No, sir. Hisself. He talked to hisself and I used to listen ...

Scene Seven

(Washroom, Gallinger's Hospital at night. Some light stays on BEATTY while also rising around the urinals. There is now a pattern of bars in the light. During the following speech, BEATTY slowly moves down towards EZRA.)

EZRA: *(Staring straight ahead.)* They put me in a cage. At Pisa. I do remember that. Of course I remember that. Bars all around me. At Pisa. *(Quietly: a statement.)* Help. They covered the bars with steel netting—because they were afraid that someone would come and rescue me. Help. *(He punctuates the following by banging on the top of the urinal.)* That some friends *(Bang.)* from somewhere *(Bang.)* would swoop down out of the hills above Pisa *(Bang.)* just the way they rescued Benito Muss! Ben Muss. Came down out of the air, grabbed him and ran! *(Bang.)* Aiuto! Help!

(Lights become bright, white, while bar pattern fades. The sound of running water in constant flow, as in urinals.)

BEATTY: Some person call for help in here?

EZRA: Some person is takin' a leak in here. Get out.

BEATTY: I can't get out. It's my job to come in.

(BEATTY begins to inspect the urinals and stalls, while humming the tune, "Banks of the Wabash.")

EZRA: You lookin' for someone? Or something?

BEATTY: Someone called "help."

EZRA: You don't say.

BEATTY: Yes. I think it was maybe you. But I'll go on lookin' anyway. For interest's sake. *(Pause.)* You sure do take a long leak, Mister.

EZRA: I was attempting to take a short one, but you came in and destroyed my concentration.

BEATTY: Why'd you call for help?

EZRA: I did not call for help!

BEATTY: Must've been the taps, then. There's no one else here but you and me. An' them. *(Moves to the sinks.)* Course, they're all takin' a leak ... *(Pause.)* Would it help if I made them run awhile, proper?

(Begins to turn on the taps. The sound of running tap water.)

EZRA: Thank you. *(BEATTY turns on more taps.)* Thank you. *(More taps.)* Thank you. *(Panic.)* Thank you!

(BEATTY turns off the taps while singing softly to himself.)

BEATTY: *(Singing.)*
Oh, the moonlight's fair
Tonight along the Wabash,
From the fields there comes
The smell of new mown hay.

Through the sycamores
The candle lights are gleaming,
On the banks of the Wabash,
Far away ...

EZRA: *(Pause. Quietly.)* Well ...

BEATTY: *(Finishing the song.)* Far ... far ... away ...

EZRA: *(Coming out from behind the urinal.)* I suppose you wouldn't happen to have a cigarette—

BEATTY: Patients aren't allowed to smoke.

EZRA: *(Chuckles.)* They can burn, but not smoke. Is that it?

BEATTY: *(Offers cigarettes.)* Here. I'm not supposed to smoke on the job, neither. But I won't tell if you won't.

EZRA: Oh, I won't tell. *(Takes a cigarette.)* Thanks.

> *(BEATTY lights EZRA's cigarette and his own. They take the first drag in silence.)*

Perhaps it would interest you to know who I am.

BEATTY: No. I don't ask names.

EZRA: So. It doesn't interest you. That's a unique experience. *(Pause.)* Tell me what time it is.

BEATTY: Night-time.

EZRA: I know it's night-time, you maniac. What is the hour?

BEATTY: I don't know. You think I carry a watch?

EZRA: Don't they ever turn the lights out around this place?

BEATTY: No, sir.

EZRA: The least they could do is turn them down. It's undignified.

Scene Eight

> *(Courtroom. Lights come up on the whole Court. The washroom lights slowly fade to match them.)*

JUDGE: *(Addressing a point to his right where BEATTY is supposed to be standing in front of the jury box.)* So, Mister Beatty, you met often with Mister Pound in this fashion?

BEATTY: *(Still near EZRA, looking at him sadly.)* Yessir. Most nights he was there.

JUDGE: And you spoke—or rather he spoke of the situation regarding this trial?

BEATTY: Yes. And very bitter.

JUDGE: So I believe. Well, Mister Beatty, I can see I will have to excuse you from this case.

BEATTY: Yessir. Your Honor.

(With one last look at EZRA, BEATTY slowly exits.)

JUDGE: Do any of the others know Mister Pound? *(Pause.)* Very well. Let us proceed. We have chosen the jury. Mister Matlack, Mister Anderson, have you any further questions regarding this choice?

MATLACK: *(Rises.)* We are satisfied, Your Honor. *(Sits.)*

JUDGE: Mister Cornell?

CORNELL: *(Rises.)* I am satisfied, Your Honor. *(Sits.)*

JUDGE: Swear the jury.

(CLERK exits right.)

EZRA: *(Moving over to below the JUDGE.)* You didn't ask me, you son-of-a-bitch! You didn't ask if I'm satisfied! It's my goddamned jury!

JUDGE: *(Bangs gavel.)* Mister Cornell, would you call your first witness?

(EZRA, in disgust, starts towards his stool, but is stopped by what he hears CORNELL say.)

CORNELL: *(Rises.)* Thank you, Your Honor. I call Doctor Muncie.

(CORNELL sits. MUNCIE enters from the left and stands in front of the witness chair. The CLERK enters from the right and swears him in with the following exchange, which is overridden by the next exchange between EZRA and CORNELL.)

CLERK: Raise your right hand. Do you swear to tell the truth, the whole truth and nothing but the truth, so help you God?

MUNCIE: I do.

CLERK: Be seated and state your full name.

MUNCIE: Doctor Wendell Muncie.

EZRA: *(Approaching CORNELL.)* Did he say Muncie?

CORNELL: *(Addressing EZRA's chair.)* Yes. And be quiet, Mister Pound. This man is about to testify in your behalf.

EZRA: You know of course that he's a hangman.

(CORNELL makes a shushing gesture. EZRA, in disgust, goes to sit on his stool.)

CORNELL: Doctor Muncie, will you state your profession?

MUNCIE: I am a psychiatrist.

CORNELL: Will you tell me what institution you are connected with in your practice?

MUNCIE: I am Associate Professor of Psychiatry at the Johns Hopkins Hospital, and consulting psychiatrist at several other hospitals.

CORNELL: When did you first examine the defendant here, Mister Pound?

MUNCIE: December 13th, 1945, roughly two-and-a-half months ago.

CORNELL: And where was he then confined?

MUNCIE: He was in the Gallinger Hospital.

CORNELL: Were you attempting, at that time, to define his illness?

MUNCIE: Yes.

CORNELL: Will you state what symptoms you found in Mister Pound?

MUNCIE: Yes, sir. May I have reference to some notes?

CORNELL: *(With a glance at the JUDGE.)* Certainly.

(MUNCIE takes notes from an inside jacket pocket and unfolds them. EZRA swivels on his stool to look at him, and then, during the following, rises to stand stage left of him, trying to read the notes.)

MUNCIE: Well, there are a number of things that I—

CORNELL: *(Indicating the microphone, stage right of MUNCIE.)* Doctor Muncie, perhaps you had better turn so the jury can hear you clearly.

MUNCIE: Yes, sir.

(He turns, right, to the microphone. EZRA shrugs and walks around to also be on MUNCIE's right.)

There are a number of things which attracted my attention in examining Mister Pound ...

CORNELL: Yes?

(EZRA shushes Cornell. He wants to hear this.)

MUNCIE: Yes. Well. He has a number of fixed ideas ...

(Each of EZRA's interruptions occur as MUNCIE consults his notes.)

EZRA: Fixed? You mean stuck? Or you mean they've been mended?

MUNCIE: These fixed ideas are either clearly delusional or verging on the delusional. One I might speak of, for instance: he believes he has been designated to save the Constitution of the United States for the people of the United States ...

EZRA: And if I don't—who will?

MUNCIE: I will come back to this item in a minute. *(Coughs.)* Secondly, he has the feeling that he has the key to the peace of the world through the writings of Confucius, which he translated into Italian and into English, and that if this book had been given proper circulation, the Axis would not have been formed and we would be at peace now, and a great deal of trouble could have been avoided in the past, and this becomes his blueprint for the world order for the future.

EZRA: And why not? Confucius was our sage forebear. No matter what language you have him in ...

MUNCIE: Thirdly, Mister Pound has a hatred of bureaucrats which goes back a long way ...

EZRA: Goddamn right it does.

MUNCIE: And one may conclude that his saving of the Constitution draws a clear distinction between the rights of the people and those who govern people. So much for the rather fixed ideas he holds ...

CORNELL: You have more, Doctor Muncie?

MUNCIE: Oh, yes, indeed. Indeed, more. Mister Pound shows a remarkable grandiosity.

(General laughter in the court.)

He feels that he has no peer in the intellectual world.

EZRA: Haven't.

MUNCIE: Although, he concedes that one or two persons he has assisted might, on occasion, do as good work as he did.

EZRA: Joyce. Eliot. On occasion.

MUNCIE: This all sounds as if it was clear cut ...

EZRA: Like a diamond.

(During the following, EZRA will feel the increasing need to empty his bladder. He wants to listen, but must eventually move over to

the urinal. While he makes his way over, the lights slowly fade on the Court, but become brighter in the urinal area.)

MUNCIE: But it is not clear cut—and the case from a psychiatric standpoint has a remarkable vagueness. In addition to the vagueness, there is a considerable "distractibility." For instance, if Mister Pound is asked a specific question as to a specific situation, he begins to make an answer and then, all of a sudden, is making a statement about a number of topics which may be clear in his mind, but cannot be clear in the examiner's mind. There is a great "push" ...

(EZRA, by now at the urinal strains to start the stream.)

... and then a condition we refer to as "stupor" when nothing comes. He just ... holds his head ...

EZRA: Aiuto ... help.

MUNCIE: But nothing comes. *(Pause.)* At these times, he has complained of a feeling of ...

EZRA: Emptiness ...

MUNCIE: Emptiness in the forehead. Or a feeling of ...

EZRA: Pressure.

MUNCIE: ... pressure in the forehead.

EZRA: *(Release.)* Agh!

Scene Nine

(Gallinger Hospital washroom. BEATTY enters.)

EZRA: What place is this?

BEATTY: The john.

EZRA: Which john? Where?

BEATTY: The one in Washington, D.C.

EZRA: Ah, yes. That john. Sometime after midnight, I surmise.

BEATTY: That's right.

EZRA: *(Coming out from behind the urinal.)* Are you afraid of the dark, Mister Beatty?

BEATTY: Oh—I guess it depends where the darkness is.

EZRA: Yes. *(Pause.)* Myself, I'm half afraid of darkness, half afraid of light.

BEATTY: Twilight, we call that.

EZRA: Yes. I'm afraid of the twilight. Why?

(Lights begin to fade and show a bar pattern.)

BEATTY: That's when most of us gets lost. I guess.

EZRA: They want to kill me, you know. They say I've committed treason ... They put me in a cage. At Pisa. Pisa, which is in Italy.

BEATTY: I've heard of it. The Leaning Tower and all—

EZRA: That's right. There was a mountain, too. Much taller than the tower. And they both leaned over my cage. I turned myself in, you understand. There I was. An American. You see. And the war was over. May, 1945. And so—I came down. Out of my house. My house was on a hilltop. Sant'Ambrogio. And I ... I came from the house and gave myself up to the first American I saw. He was black. He was a Negro. And I said: "I am ... I am ..."

BEATTY: I don't ask names.

EZRA: I am I. "It is I," I said. And he said "yes." He agreed, you see. He knew it was me. So, I turned myself in ... and they put me in a cage. They said I was a traitor. But I had turned myself in. Smiling. *(Pause.)* The cage had seventeen bars. No roof. No other floor but one of concrete. Nowhere to rest. And nothing but a bucket. All because they said I was a traitor.

(Light begins to intensify in urinal area and slowly comes up to usual level in the whole Court. The bar pattern remains on EZRA.)

And all night long ... a great, white searchlight lit me in my cage. And all day long, the sun refused to darken. And no one came—but my wife. And here I am. Now—I am here.

BEATTY: Yessir. I can see you.

(Bar pattern fades. BEATTY slowly exits during the following:)

Scene Ten

(Courtroom.)

MUNCIE: That is how the patient appears to me, now. Vague, distraught—relying almost exclusively on confrontation.

EZRA: *(Vague.)* What?

CORNELL: Doctor Muncie, I wonder if you could go into a little more detail about Mister Pound's predicament, and how well he understands it.

MUNCIE: Well, he has two minds about that.

> *(EZRA slowly returns to his cot and sits.)*

At times he believes he could persuade any jury, anywhere, that he has not committed treason. At other times he states categorically that he is not of sound mind. The latter, I would concur with.

CORNELL: Did you at any time ascertain whether he understood the nature of the offence?

MUNCIE: Whether he understands the meaning of treason or not, I do not know. He certainly denies that he committed anything like treason, in his view, against the people of the United States.

CORNELL: Doctor Muncie, will you tell the jury what is your opinion as to Mister Pound's ability to understand the meaning of a trial under this indictment for treason—and, particularly, his ability to consult with counsel in order to formulate a defense to the indictment.

MUNCIE: I think he is not capable of doing any of those things.

CORNELL: Thank you, Doctor Muncie. I have no more questions.

> *(CORNELL returns to his place and sits.)*

JUDGE: Your witness, Mister Matlack.

MATLACK: *(Coming forward.)* Thank you, Your Honor. Doctor Muncie, did you go into his history when you went to interview Mister Pound?

MUNCIE: I had a statement from Mister Cornell, the defendant's counsel. He pretty well summed up Mister Pound's situation to the time—to the date of his being taken prisoner in Italy and being brought here.

MATLACK: Did you have any history besides that?

MUNCIE: Yes. I had newspaper clippings and general writings—you know—from people more qualified than I am to judge his literary ability.

MATLACK: By newspaper clippings, you refer—Doctor Muncie—to those contained in the petition filed here by Mister Cornell?

MUNCIE: Yes, sir.

MATLACK: Did you have any other history given to you by Mister Pound as to his condition?

MUNCIE: No, sir.

MATLACK: Did you have any information furnished to you by Mister Pound as to his childhood—where he was born, for instance?

MUNCIE: I had only secondary information—hospital records at Gallinger. But these were rather complete.

MATLACK: Was he able to discuss that intelligently with you? The distant past, I mean?

MUNCIE: He gave me some of the facts.

(During the following, the lights partly dim except on EZRA's area, and during EZRA's first speech, MUNCIE will slowly leave the witness chair, walk down, pick up EZRA's stool, place it left of the cot and sit.)

Scene Eleven

(EZRA's room at Gallinger Hospital.)

EZRA: Born, October 30th, 1885, at Hailey, Idaho, in the United States of Am ... urrr ... ica! Had a father called *Homer* and a mother called *Isabel Weston Pound*. Yessir—born at the end of a disorderly trek of four or five generations across the whole teeming continent ... Hailey, Idaho was five-thousand feet above sea level, Muncie, and the height nearly drove my mother crazy. Lookin' down, you might say, did not agree with her. So she drug us off to New York City, where she'd been born and the height of things was tolerable.

(MUNCIE takes a notebook out of his inside pocket and leafs through it.)

MUNCIE: "Drug" you off?

EZRA: Hauled us, Doctor Muncie. You never been hauled against your will from one place to another?

MUNCIE: I guess not.

EZRA: Isabel Weston hauled us through a blizzard, winter of '87.

MUNCIE: You were still just a baby then, Mister Pound.

EZRA: You think that makes a difference? I was forcibly removed from the place where I was born.

MUNCIE: Was your mother's health improved by this move?

EZRA: I'd say her health was improved by the presence of civilization. Next thing I knew we were living in Philadelphia, home of the Constitution of the United States.

MUNCIE: I thought the Constitution was housed here in Washington, D.C., Mister Pound.

EZRA: Oh, yes. That's where they keep it, now. But it was born in Philadelphia, and afterwards—like me from Hailey, Idaho—they drug it off—they hauled it off and maimed it. Took it to Washington, D.C. and did it in. Mister Jefferson would never have allowed such a thing.

MUNCIE: Do you think you were "maimed," Mister Pound, when your mother took you away from Hailey?

EZRA: Me and the Constitution: one and the same. But I recovered.

(EZRA rises and wanders down stage.)

MUNCIE: I see. *(Pause.)* Are you restless, Mister Pound?

EZRA: Maybe. What I'm doing is coming over here to look out this window. I trust a madman may do that. Even crazy people like to see the view, from time to time.

MUNCIE: Of course.

EZRA: You think I'm crazy, Muncie?

MUNCIE: *(The diplomat.)* I shouldn't say so. No.

EZRA: But you will say so—when you have to?

MUNCIE: When I have to, Mister Pound?

EZRA: You heard me.

(MUNCIE turns the pages of his notebook.)

I make you nervous, don't I?

MUNCIE: Not in the least.

EZRA: You think I'm violent.

MUNCIE: I have no evidence of that.

EZRA: You want some? Violence?

MUNCIE: Mister Pound …

EZRA: So … tell me what you do want?

MUNCIE: I want to know about Italy.

EZRA: Shaped like a boot. The boot, I always thought, of a highwayman. A buccaneer's boot. An early eighteenth century boot—ineffably romantic. The hat that goes with such a boot would have a feather in it.

MUNCIE: You lived there, in Italy, for a good many years.

EZRA: I went there first in 1908. To Venice. *(Pause.)* I will die in Venice, Doctor Muncie, or I will not die at all. It is God's best gift to man.

MUNCIE: I hadn't thought you had been in Italy ever since 1908, Mister Pound.

EZRA: Oh, no. I didn't go there to live until 1924.

MUNCIE: And that would have been at Rapallo.

EZRA: *(Wandering towards stage right.)* Rapallo on the Via Reggio.

MUNCIE: You were there when you were arrested?

EZRA: I was not arrested. I gave myself up. To a black man. A Negro.

MUNCIE: But you gave yourself up at Rapallo?

EZRA: Almost. I was living then—in May of last year—at Sant'Ambrogio—above Rapallo—with my wife in the house of Miss Olga Rudge, the mother of my daughter, Mary.

> *(DOROTHY enters from stage right, carrying a book.)*

We were there because …

DOROTHY: *(Addressing EZRA's empty chair down right.)* Ezra?

MUNCIE: Yes?

DOROTHY: Ezra?

MUNCIE: Mister Pound?

EZRA: Go away.

MUNCIE: I beg your pardon?

EZRA: *(Walking to his empty chair.)* Go away.

DOROTHY: Go away? Where? You know I can't do that.

EZRA: Get on a train. Go back to England. What do you mean, you can't do that.

> *(As lights dim centre stage, MUNCIE crosses back up to the witness chair. Lights come up fully down right. Violin music is heard off right.)*

Scene Twelve

(EZRA's house, Rapallo.)

DOROTHY: I can't do that because I won't, Ezra. Damn you. Damn you.

EZRA: Ah, the lady Dorothy at last said "damn."

DOROTHY: I'd say worse if I could think of it. You bastard! You've given my child to her.

EZRA: Well ... you—

DOROTHY: Don't you dare say I didn't want a child. Don't you dare say that. We had no child because you wanted none. You—not me. You didn't want them cluttering up your precious freedom. Now, Olga Rudge is going to have the child I wanted—and you behave as if it was her due! Damn you—Goddamn you. *(Pause.)* Oh, that bloody music! *Stop!*

> *(Throws the book off right. There is the sound of a window breaking. Violin stops.)*

EZRA: You threw Mister Eliot's book at Olga Rudge—

DOROTHY: Good! And if "Mister" Eliot was here, I'd throw him at her, too.

EZRA: Tut, tut! Old Possum through a window ... ? Cut and broken? Broken and cut and bleeding? In the street? The Possum? What a savage image. Hah!

DOROTHY: Oh, yes, Ezra—everything's just a scream here, isn't it?

EZRA: Well, you must admit ...

DOROTHY: I don't have to admit a goddamn thing. It isn't me who does the "lying" around here—you should pardon the pun. Come to think of it, I'd like to throw all the rest of your protégés out that window— the composers—the poets—*(Shouting into wings, right.)*—the b-loody pregnant violinists!*—the sculptors and the painters ...

EZRA: You're a painter, Dorothy.

DOROTHY: Yes, but I'm not your goddamn protégé! Your protégés at least get pregnant. *(Weeps in anger.)*

EZRA: Don't cry ...

DOROTHY: I'm not crying. I'm furious. It's just occurred to me that if this child is going to be born in July, then it must have been conceived in October—on your birthday. On your birthday—while I celebrated you—you bedded Olga. And gave her *my child.*

EZRA: *(Unemotional, factual.)* I didn't—we didn't mean to, you know. It just happened.

> *(During the following, the lights slowly dim around DOROTHY and rise over the whole court. MATLACK crosses to MUNCIE, who is still in the witness chair.)*

DOROTHY: Happened? "Just happened?" Ezra, if I could believe that anything about you "just happened," I'd join the Catholic Church and become a nun. I'd crawl on my hands and knees all the way to Rome. I'd ...

Scene Thirteen

(Courtroom.)

MATLACK: How did you find his memory, Doctor Muncie? Was his memory "peculiar"?

MUNCIE: His memory, far as I could find, was all right ...

EZRA: Goddamn right it was all right. Chapter and verse. Except for ...

MUNCIE: Except for a substantive period in the prison at Pisa. At Pisa there appears to have been a blackout of memory.

MATLACK: Ah, yes. Yes. Yes ... a "blackout of memory" ... at Pisa. *(Pause.)* Doctor Muncie—don't you think it would be normal for a person—having been charged with treason—to be under emotional stress?

MUNCIE: I wouldn't know, Mister Matlack. I ... I mean, I've never ... I mean—

MATLACK: It's all right, Doctor. We know you have never been charged with treason.

(Laughter in the court.)

MUNCIE: Still, in all honesty, I would think such a serious charge would be an incentive to keep your thoughts about you. But the answer is: I don't know.

MATLACK: Has the nature of the charge, Doctor Muncie—namely, that of treason—had an effect on Mister Pound's mental condition?

MUNCIE: No, sir.

MATLACK: Did you talk to Mister Pound about the charge of treason?

MUNCIE: Yes.

EZRA: Liar.

MATLACK: Did he tell you that he had been indicted in 1943 as a result of his radio broadcasts?

MUNCIE: No ...

EZRA: *(Rises, moves closer up towards the witness chair.)* Liar.

MUNCIE: ... that came to him as a surprise, later on.

MATLACK: I see. And yet we know that on the 4th of August, 1943,

Mister Pound wrote to Francis Biddle, who was then Attorney General of the United States, claiming, and I quote: "I do not believe that the simple fact of speaking over the radio, wherever placed, can in itself constitute treason. I think that must depend on what is said and on the motives for speaking ..."

EZRA: *(Closer to the witness chair.)* Damn right—and I've said so all along.

MATLACK: Mister Pound had this letter forwarded to Mister Biddle ...

EZRA: Francis Biddle—that's right. Attorney General of the United States ...

MATLACK: ... had it forwarded through the Swiss Legation in Rome ...

EZRA: ... of America!

MATLACK: ... Clearly, the letter was written in reply to the charges of treason brought against him when he was indicted by a Federal Grand Jury in the United States District Court, District of Columbia, on the 26th of July, 1943. *(Thrusts papers at MUNCIE, who ignores them.)* Mister Pound's letter ...

EZRA: Letter! What letter?

MATLACK: ... his letter to the Attorney General goes on at some length—detailing why, in his view, he should not be charged with treason and yet you claim that Mister Pound was unaware he would be charged with treason and that—in your words—the charges came to him "as a surprise later on."

EZRA: *(To MUNCIE.)* Say " yes."

MUNCIE: That is my belief.

MATLACK: Could you put a date on "later on"?

MUNCIE: Oh ...

EZRA: *(Close to MUNCIE.)* Careful, Muncie. Careful.

MUNCIE: Perhaps in May of last year.

MATLACK: May, 1945?

EZRA: That's right. Absolutely.

MUNCIE: Yes. Somewhere between May and October of 1945.

MATLACK: Which is, very roughly speaking, the same period—or part of the same period—when you say Mister Pound suffered his "loss of memory."

MUNCIE: *(Pause.)* Yes.

EZRA: Yes!

MATLACK: Do you think he understands the nature of the charge against him? That he can be tried for the crime of treason?

EZRA: Say "no," you idiot.

MUNCIE: Yes.

EZRA: *No!*

> *(EZRA moves up to the witness microphone and begins broadcasting.)*

Every hour that you go on with this war is an hour lost to you and your children! And every sane act that you commit is committed in homage to Mussolini and Hitler. They are your leaders, however much you think you are conducted by Roosevelt or Churchill ...

> *(MUNCIE rises and manages to begin to move EZRA down to his centre stage area. The lights begin now to dim on the rest of the court.)*

Scene Fourteen

(EZRA's room, Gallinger Hospital.)

MUNCIE: Mister Pound ...

EZRA: *(Winding down.)* You follow Mussolini or Hitler in every constructive act ... of your ... government ...

MUNCIE: Mister Pound—please—be seated. Please be seated.

EZRA: *(Breathless.)* You are not going to win this war. You are not going to win.

MUNCIE: Please. You must attempt—you must try to contain yourself. For your own sake.

EZRA: Oh—I don't matter. I don't matter. It's the words that matter.

MUNCIE: Mister Pound, don't you think you should sit down. You're completely out of breath.

EZRA: Yes. I ... In fact, I ...

MUNCIE: Here, let me help you. *(MUNCIE helps EZRA sit on his cot.)* You lie on the bed.

EZRA: Not down. I won't lie down.

MUNCIE: No, no. But you can lie on the bed—get your feet up—there ...

EZRA: Ah ...

MUNCIE: You'll be more comfortable like this ... sit up a little ... there ... How's that? Better?

EZRA: Yes. *(Winding down further.)* Thank you. Yes.

MUNCIE: *(Getting a glass of water from EZRA's table, from down right.)* You mustn't get so excited, Mister Pound. Here ... drink this. Catch your breath ...

EZRA: What is this?

MUNCIE: Water. Drink it.

EZRA: No. It's been poisoned.

MUNCIE: *(Laughs.)* Nonsense—

EZRA: How do you know? Were you here when that glass got filled?

MUNCIE: No, I wasn't. But I can assure you—this water has not been poisoned.

EZRA: Prove it. Drink it.

MUNCIE: All right. *(Takes a sip.)* There.

EZRA: *(Drinks eagerly.)* Ahhhh.

> *(EZRA hands the glass to MUNCIE.)*

MUNCIE: Good. *(Takes glass to the table.)*

EZRA: I would like a cigarette.

MUNCIE: All right.

> *(He takes out a pack and offers EZRA a cigarette.)*

EZRA: I thought it was against the rules.

MUNCIE: It is against the rules. Here ...

> *(MUNCIE lights EZRA's cigarette.)*

The thing is, Mister Pound, nearly everything you do is against the rules, one way or another.

EZRA: *(Pleased.)* You think so?

MUNCIE: Yes.

EZRA: Good.

MUNCIE: *(Crossing to a window and looking out.)* I've never been to

Italy, Mister Pound. Are the winters there like this—with all this snow and slush? Does it get as dark as this in the afternoon?

EZRA: In the wintertime it rains. Mostly, that is the difference. Of course, it snows in the mountains. Northward to Austria.

MUNCIE: Yes. *(Pause.)* Mister Pound, may I ask you, do you have a faith to sustain you?

EZRA: *(Chuckles.)* Only that I'm here. Alive. I know that for sure—

MUNCIE: Yes. But—God. I mean, God.

EZRA: *(Shifting higher in the cot.)* Doctor Muncie, either you must take me for some kind of fool, or I must take you for one.

MUNCIE: I only meant—

EZRA: You only meant: had I thrown myself to the wolves of religion. You sound like Mister Eliot—or worse, you sound like Pius XII. No, I do not have a God. But I believe in moral precepts—I believe the spirit can rise above itself—I believe we can be better—or be worse— the moral man's life reflects the universal order. That's Confucius. Confucius never speaks of God, but he speaks a great deal of the universal order. I call that "God." Or, I would, if "God" was in my vocabulary. This is where Mister Eliot and I were much at odds. The relationship of Christianity to Confucianism. The names of things, you see. The naming. The problem—hah!—of the different brands of Christianity! The commercial value of the brands of religion—the language of the god-names! Agh! Poor old Possum—all caught up in the naming of his gawd. *(Laughs, then sobers.)* On the other hand, I will say this: when a man loses reverence, he loses a great deal. *(Pause.)* Mind you, there's reverence and there's reverence. And then there's worship. It's worship that troubles me. I never could bend the knee. *(Pause. He is in reverie.)* We have too many languages. Too many languages. I cannot be expected to learn them all.

MUNCIE: Of course not.

EZRA: Too many languages—not enough words … *(Pause.)* You have no compunction, Doctor? You are not compelled?

MUNCIE: Compunction? Compelled, Mister Pound?

EZRA: To speak. To speak. To say?

MUNCIE: I cannot answer that. I feel the need, of course, sometimes. Sometimes, I want to shout—

EZRA: But you don't.

MUNCIE: I'm afraid not. No.

EZRA: You should. It would do you good. *(Pause.)* The Possum once asked me pointedly what I "believe." I said to him, "Read Confucius! Read Mister Ovid! They can do no harm to the intelligent. And the unintelligent may be damned ...! I tell you what I'd do," I said. "I'd erect a temple to Artemis in Park Lane!" He didn't care for that, Old Poss. So he went back into the fold—the "flock"—where, instead of disguising himself as a sheep, he disguised himself as a corpse.

MUNCIE: You seem not to care for Mister Eliot.

EZRA: I love him. Don't you know he's one of my sons?

MUNCIE: I see.

EZRA: The whole of 20th century English literature is mine. You didn't know that, Muncie? Eliot, Joyce and Yeats: all mine. And Mauberley. The whole of 20th century literature—all—to say nothing of the past, which I've reclaimed ...

MUNCIE: I had thought Hugh Selwyn Mauberley was a fiction, Mister Pound.

EZRA: And he is—he is. So, doesn't that tell you about the rest of them!

Scene Fifteen

(Courtroom. Lights rise fully.)

MATLACK: *(With his back to the empty witness chair.)* Grandiosity, Doctor. What do you mean when you say he shows "grandiosity"? What does it mean, exactly?

MUNCIE: *(Staring at EZRA.)* It means an exaggerated opinion of one's self.

MATLACK: Is that a sign of insanity?

EZRA: No.

MATLACK: Doctor Muncie?

MUNCIE: *(Walking slowly back to sit in witness chair.)* If it gets out of bounds, it is. Yes.

MATLACK: And when does it get out of bounds, in your opinion?

MUNCIE: It gets out of bounds in certain paranoid states.

JUDGE: In fact, this is very common to paranoia, isn't it?

MUNCIE: Yes, Your Honor.

MATLACK: *(Facing MUNCIE.)* In connection with the charge of treason, did Mister Pound discuss with you his activities in broadcasting?

MUNCIE: Yes. He told me about his broadcasts.

MATLACK: Yes. But with respect to treason?

MUNCIE: He said that they did not constitute treason.

MATLACK: Might it not be, however, that he believed he was not legally liable for treason?

MUNCIE: If you were to take out the word "legally," I would agree with you.

MATLACK: Wouldn't that opinion indicate he was not of sound mind?

MUNCIE: *(Happily, thinking MATLACK has changed his opinion.)* Yes.

    (EZRA sits up and listens.)

MATLACK: Yet, you have already answered the question as to whether he understands the charge he is under … in the affirmative.

MUNCIE: *(Taken aback.)* Yes.

MATLACK: And that he understood he was being brought over here to be tried on that charge.

MUNCIE: Yes.

MATLACK: So, will you explain, please, to the jury why you think Ezra Pound is unable to consult with Counsel.

    (EZRA moves up to the steps leading to the witness area.)

MUNCIE: Well … because … *(His voice drops.)* Because …

MATLACK: Yes?

JUDGE: Speak louder, Doctor Muncie.

MUNCIE: Yes, Your Honor.

MATLACK: *(Pause.)* Have you forgotten the question, Doctor?

MUNCIE: No.

MATLACK: Then may we have an answer, please.

MUNCIE: I have no doubt—I have absolutely no doubt that Mister Pound's Counsel would have the same experience I had, namely—

MATLACK: Yes?

MUNCIE: When you try to pin him down to anything, you are left out on a limb because of his vagueness and distractibility. He—

MATLACK: All you have to do, Doctor Muncie, is recall Mister Pound's attention to the subject under discussion. I mean—I presume you did that. I presume you attempted to draw Mister Pound back to the subject at hand.

MUNCIE: *(Angry.)* It is impossible to stay on the subject. When you end up—there isn't any coherent statement.

> *(EZRA sits on the steps.)*

MATLACK: No coherent statement.

MUNCIE: *(Going too far.)* No intelligent thought.

> *(EZRA turns to glare at MUNCIE.)*

MATLACK: No intell ... No intelligent thought. Well, well, well ... *(Pause.)* He answered your questions?

MUNCIE: Yes. But ... no.

MATLACK: He did or he didn't, Doctor Muncie, answer your questions.

MUNCIE: No. No. When I might say, Mister Pound, you are concerned about the Constitution ...

EZRA: A beautiful document. Yes.

MUNCIE: Tell me which items you want to defend specifically.

EZRA: The President is a Magistrate with delegated powers.

MUNCIE: *(Throwing up his hands.)* The President is a Magistrate with delegated powers. And that was all I could get.

MATLACK: You think that is not a fair description of the Presidency?

MUNCIE: That isn't the point.

MATLACK: But the Presidency is described in the Constitution, is it not?

EZRA: Yes.

MUNCIE: Yes.

MATLACK: And you had asked that Mister Pound discuss which items were of interest to him?

> *(EZRA nods.)*

MUNCIE: Yes.

MATLACK: And he gave you an answer.

MUNCIE: It was not an answer!

MATLACK: What, then, was it?

MUNCIE: *(Extremely flustered.)* A ... it was a ... he was paraphrasing. Summing up. Taking things out of context.

MATLACK: But the paraphrase in question—"the President is a Magistrate with delegated powers"—is pertinent to the Constitution, is it not?

MUNCIE: *(Testy.)* Yes. Yes. Yes.

JUDGE: Mister Matlack, however proud I am of the Constitution, I do not regard its contents as the subject of this hearing.

(EZRA rises, glaring at the JUDGE.)

MATLACK: *(Tired.)* I am attempting, Your Honor, to establish that, when it is said that Mister Pound is incapable of conferring with Counsel—it very well might be that Counsel is incapable of conferring with Mister Pound.

EZRA: Damn right.

JUDGE: I see. *(With good humour.)* And, of course, you propose this scenario with all due respect to Mister Cornell's intelligence.

(EZRA moves up onto the JUDGE's level, watching him.)

MATLACK: But, of course, Your Honor.

JUDGE: I should not approve of what you said unless there was some respect in it.

MATLACK: Yes, Your Honor.

EZRA: *(Into JUDGE's ear.)* Buzz, buzz ...

(The JUDGE idly shoos a fly away during the following.)

JUDGE: Well, I would like to propose that your point concerning this matter is now well established, Mister Matlack, and that you should proceed with a new line of questioning.

MATLACK: Thank you, Your Honor. Doctor Muncie, what is your observation regarding Ezra Pound's intelligence?

EZRA: Buzz, buzz ... Watch it, Muncie.

MUNCIE: I think it is not too high—too great—at the present time because there are difficulties with his thinking process.

(EZRA starts down the steps towards the witness chair. The JUDGE waves another fly away and then looks around his desk, trying to spot it.)

MATLACK: But his memory is good enough? You have testified that he answered questions about his past with almost remarkable recall: dates, addresses, states of mind, the people in his past, et cetera. And all correctly?

EZRA: Damn right.

> *(The JUDGE picks up his gavel, thinking he's seen the fly on his desk.)*

MUNCIE: Yes. Any problem with Mister Pound's memory, so far as I can determine, has to do with last summer—the period of his detention at Pisa ...

> *(The JUDGE, trying to kill the fly, bangs his gavel. The whole Court turns to look at him ... including EZRA.)*

MUNCIE: *(Weakly.)* ... in Italy.

> *(The JUDGE becomes aware that he has accidentally stopped proceedings. He collects himself.)*

JUDGE: Thank you gentlemen. There will now be a fifteen minute recess. Court will be reconvened at 11:15. *(Bangs the gavel.)*

CLERK: All rise.

> *(The members of the COURT, except for CORNELL, rise and file out. EZRA crosses to his chair down right. CORNELL approaches him.)*

Scene Sixteen

(Courthouse corridor and washroom.)

CORNELL: We can take a short stroll now, Mister Pound. You want a washroom?

> *(He guides EZRA left to the urinal area.)*

EZRA: What I would like is to take a leak into the Grand Canyon. From the top, you understand.

> *(When they reach stage left, EZRA goes in behind the urinal.)*

Urinalli ... Monumenti ... You know, these tall white basins are just an extension of the male urinary tract. You ever think of that, Cornell? Just an extension of the urinary tract. Surely there can be no other symbol that shows as well as this what it means to be a man ... Ahhh ... the great flood and flow of male urine—symbolic of the great flood and flow of sperm from all the men who ever were ... You ever consider that, Cornell?

CORNELL: No, sir.

EZRA: *(Patting the urinal.)* These are the rivers up which we struggle in order to fertilize the spawn of potential nations. *(Change of tone as he moves out from behind the urinal.)* I should like to have been on the stand to answer some of Matlack's questions. You can see it in his eyes—he hates me.

CORNELL: Oh, I'm not so sure he hates you, Mister Pound. He has his job to do.

EZRA: You think so?

CORNELL: Yessir.

EZRA: Well, and who pays him for that? His job.

CORNELL: The Government, of course.

(He looks at his watch, gives a farewell salute to EZRA and exits right, as the lights dim on the rest of the Court.)

EZRA: "The Government." Of course.

(Pause. Then EZRA starts to sing softly to himself as he washes his hands. During the singing, BEATTY enters left.)

Oh, the moonlight's fair
Tonight along the Wabash
From the fields there comes
The smell of new mown hay

(All at once, he stops singing. He slumps.)

Oh …

(Slowly, he raises his head and stares at himself in the mirror.)

BEATTY: *(Pause.)* So. They want you to hang, is that it?

EZRA: Yes. That's it.

BEATTY: But you're safe here.

EZRA: I guess. Yes.

BEATTY: Yes. I guess.

EZRA: *(Continuing to stare at himself.)* You been here long?

BEATTY: All my life. So it seems.

EZRA: Tell me your name, old man.

BEATTY: Beatty. Arthur Beatty. Custodian.

(Offstage, a WOMAN is humming "Wabash" to a piano accompaniment. The lights fade to darkness. End of Act One.)

Act Two

Scene One

(Courthouse corridor. On the scrim is a gigantic close-up of EZRA. The Court is backlit and otherwise dimly seen. The RECORDER is in her place, as are MATLACK and ANDERSON. EZRA is lying on his cot, his back to the audience. Full light down stage and at the right, where two REPORTERS are on their phones, their words overlapping.)

REPORTER TWO: Doctor Wendell Muncie took the stand this morning at the trial of American poet Ezra Pound ...

REPORTER ONE: Doctor Muncie's testimony was sensational, by any standards ...

REPORTER TWO: It is expected that this morning's other witness, Doctor Winfred Overholser, will provide further information regarding the poet's alleged insanity ...

REPORTER ONE: ... Doctor Overholser, who is head of the Medical Staff at St. Elizabeth's Hospital here in Washington, is rumoured to have a trump card up his sleeve regarding Ezra Pound's mental condition ...

REPORTER TWO: Doctor Muncie looked exhausted as he left the witness stand this morning, having been grilled to a frazzle by Assistant Attorney General Isaiah Matlack ...

(The voices quieten, their words inaudible during the following:)

Scene Two

(Courtroom corridor. DEUTSCH and WILLIAMS enter and walk across the front of the stage.)

DEUTSCH: Have you had a chance to speak to Mister Pound today, Doctor Williams?

WILLIAMS: Of course not. That would be against the law. He's a prisoner.

DEUTSCH: He certainly doesn't look good.

WILLIAMS: No. Much older than his years.

DEUTSCH: He's sixty, now?

WILLIAMS: Yes. *(Musing.)* Old Ez—got old at last …

DEUTSCH: How do you mean that?

WILLIAMS: Ezra was always "old," Mister Deutsch—or seemingly old. Not in any decrepit way. He had the energy of youth long after "youth" had passed. But he was always old in his mind. The way the prophets were old. Born old …

(They are now near the REPORTERS.)

Do you need …? *(Gesturing to the phones.)*

DEUTSCH: I already have, thanks. I'll see you later, Mister Williams.

(WILLIAMS nods his goodbye and continues on up the stairs towards the Public Gallery. DEUTSCH collects the two REPORT-ERS, and they follow WILLIAMS, exiting left. As the lights come up on the whole Court, the CLERK enters and sits in his chair. The close-up of EZRA on the scrim fades.)

Scene Three

(Courtroom. Concentrated light on MATLACK and ANDERSON.)

ANDERSON: So, now we get the famous Doctor Overholser.

MATLACK: Yes. The famous Doctor Overholser, Ezra Pound's Swiss Guard. I expect he will come into Court fully armed—

ANDERSON: With all guns blazing—

MATLACK: No. No. I think not. Doctor Overholser may "pack a gat," as they say, but he keeps it well hidden.

(A TOADY enters from up left and approaches their table.)

TOADY: Mister Matlack?

MATLACK: Yes?

TOADY: I think you should know that Doctor Muncie has just gone into a huddle with Doctor Overholser …

MATLACK: Damn!

Scene Four

(A retiring room in the courthouse. Lights dim elsewhere and rise in the area of EZRA's empty court chair. The TOADY crosses down stage as OVERHOLSER enters to meet him.)

OVERHOLSER: You told him?

TOADY: Yes.

OVERHOLSER: Good. That should worry him.

TOADY: Shall I bring in Doctor Muncie?

OVERHOLSER: Yes. If you wouldn't mind.

(TOADY exits while OVERHOLSER sits in EZRA's chair.)

TOADY: *(Off.)* You may come in, Doctor Muncie.

MUNCIE: *(Off.)* Thank you.

(MUNCIE enters, followed by the TOADY with a wooden chair, which he places centre. OVERHOLSER rises.)

TOADY: Will that be all?

OVERHOLSER: Yes. Come back in seven minutes.

TOADY: Yes, Doctor.

(TOADY exits. OVERHOLSER sits again, offering MUNCIE the new chair. MUNCIE continues to stand.)

MUNCIE: Who was that?

OVERHOLSER. Just an assistant. You don't need to know his name.

MUNCIE: *(Sitting.)* Why have you summoned me?

OVERHOLSER: *(Offering a pack.)* Cigarette?

MUNCIE: Yes, but I'll smoke my own, thank you.

(They light up.)

Why have you summoned me, Doctor Overholser?

OVERHOLSER: Mostly for effect. I want Mister Matlack to worry when he gets me on the stand. I thought, if he sees us cloistered like this, he'll worry.

MUNCIE: He's already in the Court. He didn't even see me come in.

OVERHOLSER: He didn't have to see you come in. He knows you're here.

MUNCIE: *(Twigging.)* Ah, yes. The man who just left—

OVERHOLSER: Draw whatever conclusions you like, Muncie. Here we are.

MUNCIE: All right. Why?

OVERHOLSER: I did not like your performance this morning.

MUNCIE: I beg your pardon.

OVERHOLSER: I did not like your performance—the way you handled Matlack's questions. You dropped the ball, Doctor Muncie. You let him pick it up … and run with it.

MUNCIE: Well, so be it. There was nothing I could do. You don't seem to understand, Doctor Overholser. I do not concur with your analysis of this situation. It was very difficult—it was very hard for me to stand out there and say that I do concur. I know why I must concur—but I do not concur. Ezra Pound is no more crazy than you are …

OVERHOLSER: Perhaps. But I remind you, you signed the psychiatric report requested by Judge Laws, and having signed it, your concurrence is now a matter of public record.

MUNCIE: But I—

OVERHOLSER: *(Riding him down.)* Our summation, Doctor Muncie— our mutual summation—it was agreed upon.

MUNCIE: Damn you. I object to these tactics.

OVERHOLSER: Be quiet. Listen. Just listen. *(He picks up a piece of paper from the desk and reads.)* I quote, "Mister Pound is abnormally grandiose, is expansive and exuberant in manner, exhibiting pressure of speech, discursiveness and destructibility …"

MUNCIE: Yes. I said all that. I used those words. As we agreed I should.

OVERHOLSER: Perhaps. But your conviction slipped, Muncie. Your belief in these words was not entirely evident and I wonder if you are backsliding—

MUNCIE: *(Standing.)* I have nowhere to backslide from! Goddamn it! I didn't want to sign that bloody report—

OVERHOLSER: But you did. Sit down.

MUNCIE: *(Sitting.)* To save his life! Only to save his life …

OVERHOLSER: If I had been a member of the jury out there this morning, I would not have been convinced that Ezra Pound is insane. Now I have to do it all.

MUNCIE: I'm sure you're perfectly capable of that, Doctor Overholser.

OVERHOLSER: Don't take a slam at me, Muncie. We're all here for the same thing. And I quote, "He is, in other words, insane," unquote.

MUNCIE: All right! All right … I said the words. I don't have to win a goddamn prize for how I said them. *(Pause.)* You'd think he was your child, or your brother, or … I don't understand it. Why do you have to save him?

OVERHOLSER: Put it this way: it's a vested interest in the future.

MUNCIE: Oh? Whose future? His or yours?

OVERHOLSER: Both—and *(He smiles.)*—neither. *The* future, Doctor. Just the future.

MUNCIE: By God—I think I understand this. I'm just beginning to think I understand.

OVERHOLSER: Oh?

MUNCIE: You're saying this is a political decision. You're saying you agree with him!

OVERHOLSER: *(Pause.)* I'm not saying anything, Muncie. Nothing. And neither are you.

TOADY: *(Entering right.)* Doctor Overholser, the Court is being reconvened.

OVERHOLSER: Thank you. I'll be right there.

(TOADY exits right. OVERHOLSER stands.)

Doctor Muncie, I am—I presume—about to be called to the stand. I advise you to leave the Court. I don't want you heaving sighs all through my testimony.

MUNCIE: *(Rising.)* You make me determined to stay.

OVERHOLSER: Let me remind you that, at this very minute, the Nuremberg Trials are underway and every newspaper, every newsreel and every radio carries the message of those trials into every corner of America. In France, Laval has already been executed. In Norway, Quisling—

MUNCIE: But they were collaborators … traitors—

OVERHOLSER: Exactly. Traitors. And in England, William Joyce has been convicted of treason for no other reason than his radio broadcasts—and he has been condemned to death by hanging! Can you not take that in? If Ezra Pound goes to trial, he will hang!

MUNCIE: *(Defeated.)* Yes. I understand that.

OVERHOLSER: Then I insist you leave the Court, or you will tip our hand, however inadvertently, and give us all away.

(MUNCIE nods and exits right. As the lights come up on the whole Court, CORNELL enters to stand by his table, and OVERHOLSER moves up to join him. The JUDGE enters and stands at his desk. The CLERK rises.)

Scene Five

(Courtroom.)

CLERK: All rise.

(All but EZRA do so. The JUDGE sits and bangs his gavel.)

JUDGE: Order, please. You may be seated. *(Bangs gavel again.)* Order. Will the Clerk speak?

(As the other members of the Court sit down, the CLERK remains standing to speak.)

CLERK: Pursuant to recess, Court is now reconvened in the case of Ezra Pound.

JUDGE: Thank you. *(To CORNELL.)* Counsel, you may proceed. Your witness, I believe, Mister Cornell.

CORNELL: Thank you, Your Honor. Call Doctor Overholser.

(OVERHOLSER walks over to stand in front of the witness chair. The CLERK joins him.)

CLERK: Raise your right hand. Do you swear to tell the truth, the whole truth and nothing but the truth, so help you God?

OVERHOLSER: I do.

CLERK: Be seated, please, and state your full name.

OVERHOLSER: *(Sitting.)* My name is Winfred Overholser.

CORNELL: Doctor Overholser, will you tell me your profession at the present time?

OVERHOLSER: I am Superintendent of St. Elizabeth's Hospital in this city.

CORNELL: You are the chief medical officer of that hospital?

OVERHOLSER: Yes.

CORNELL: What is the relation of that hospital to the United States Government?

OVERHOLSER: It is operated entirely by the Federal Government under the Federal Security Agency.

CORNELL: How many patients do you have at St. Elizabeth's?

OVERHOLSER: Just under seven thousand.

(Astonishment in the Court.)

CORNELL: St. Elizabeth's is purely for mental cases?

OVERHOLSER: Yes.

CORNELL: How many doctors are serving directly under you?

OVERHOLSER: Approximately fifty, with some vacancies.

CORNELL: How long have you been in charge of that institution?

OVERHOLSER: Since October, 1937.

CORNELL: And how long have you been practicing medicine, Doctor Overholser?

OVERHOLSER: I was graduated in 1916 from Chicago University.

CORNELL: Will you tell us what examination you have made of Ezra Pound?

OVERHOLSER: Yes. *(With a sense of being well rehearsed.)* I was requested to advise the Chief Justice on the condition of the defendant, after the defendant was committed to Gallinger for observation.

CORNELL: The request came from Chief Justice Laws?

OVERHOLSER: Yes.

CORNELL: Can you tell me how many times you saw Mister Pound?

OVERHOLSER: I saw him on several occasions. I made a report on December 15th, when I had Doctor Muncie with me.

CORNELL: Did each of you examine Mister Pound alone?

OVERHOLSER: Yes. Doctor Muncie had been engaged by the defense ...

CORNELL: He was engaged by me, Doctor Overholser. You may call me by my name.

OVERHOLSER: Yes. Doctor Muncie had been engaged by you, Mister Cornell, and his examination of Ezra Pound was conducted in that light. Therefore, his examination was entirely separate from my own. Nevertheless, when we met together on the 15th of December to write our collective report, it was remarkably easy to put the report together.

CORNELL: Could you elaborate, Doctor, on what you mean by "remarkably easy"?

OVERHOLSER: Certainly. I mean that we had only to agree that we might both be talking about the same thing.

CORNELL: And you did agree?

OVERHOLSER: Yes.

CORNELL: And what was your conclusion?

OVERHOLSER: *(With a sense of definite conclusion.)* It was our opinion that the defendant, Ezra Pound, was insane and mentally unfit for trial.

(EZRA slowly wakens and sits up, facing the audience.)

CORNELL: Thank you. Now, Doctor Overholser, how long has Ezra Pound been a patient in your hospital?

OVERHOLSER: He was admitted to St. Elizabeth's on January 1st and has been there ever since—somewhat more than one month.

CORNELL: Has he been under constant observation?

OVERHOLSER: Yes.

EZRA: *(Staring straight ahead.)* I want a woman.

OVERHOLSER: I spent a long time in consultation with him just last Thursday, in fact.

EZRA: I want a woman, dammit!

CORNELL: But others, as well, other doctors at St. Elizabeth's besides yourself have been observing him?

OVERHOLSER: Yes.

EZRA: *(Rising, moving part-way up towards OVERHOLSER.)* I want a woman.

OVERHOLSER: I have before me the report made by other physicians at the hospital ...

EZRA: Now!

OVERHOLSER: ... and reading it, I see no reason to change my opinion.

EZRA: Doctor Overholser, bring me a woman!

(Lights in the Court snap to dim, except in EZRA's centre stage area where they become brighter, and there is a spotlight on OVERHOLSER.)

Scene Six

(EZRA's room at St. Elizabeth's Hospital, Washington, D.C.)

OVERHOLSER: *(Greatly amused.)* Where would you suggest I find this woman, Mister Pound.

EZRA: Go in the hall and find one! Where would you suggest I find this woman? This is a hospital, ain't it?

OVERHOLSER: *(Laughing, rising and crossing down into EZRA's area.)* Yes, sir.

EZRA: There must be ten thousand nurses out there in that corridor! I can smell 'em! Bring me one.

OVERHOLSER: Mister Pound, you can't be serious.

EZRA: I got a hard on three miles long—and if that ain't serious, you tell me.

OVERHOLSER: *(Soberly.)* I would agree. That is serious.

EZRA: So. What are you going to do about it?

OVERHOLSER: I haven't the foggiest notion, Mister Pound.

EZRA: You could buy one.

OVERHOLSER: I think not.

EZRA: What? You mean they aren't for sale?

OVERHOLSER: I dare say somewhere there are prostitutes.

EZRA: Then go and get me one.

OVERHOLSER: I cannot do that, Mister Pound. Aside from the medical ethics involved—that a doctor cannot engage in the work of a pimp— I have my reputation to think of. I can't be seen stalking about the streets of Washington looking for a prostitute.

EZRA: Why not?

OVERHOLSER: Don't you know who I am, Mister Pound?

EZRA: I hesitate to answer that question.

OVERHOLSER: I am Superintendent of this hospital.

EZRA: And I am Ezra Pound! Goddamn it! Bring me a woman!

DOROTHY: *(Off right.)* Ezra? *(She enters and approaches.)* Ezra. *(She sees OVERHOLSER.)* Hello. Which one are you?

OVERHOLSER: Doctor Overholser, ma'am.

DOROTHY: Well, I'm Mrs. Ezra Pound. How do you do.

OVERHOLSER: How do you do.

EZRA: I said a woman. Not a wife.

DOROTHY: It's good to see you, Ezra.

EZRA: Yes. Yes. Well. What are you doing here?

DOROTHY: I finally got my visa. I came as fast as I could. I'm sorry if you've been waiting.

EZRA: I wasn't aware that a visa was required in hell.

DOROTHY: I wouldn't call this hell compared to your cage in Pisa, Ezra. *(Moving about.)* In fact, this is rather a lovely room. Do you see? I've brought you flowers … *(She crosses to the stool.)* I'll put them in this glass, for now, and maybe later I can find a vase.

OVERHOLSER: That's very kind of you, Mrs. Pound.

DOROTHY: Ezra loves flowers, but you mustn't ever give him lilies. Only roses, daisies—spring flowers. Lilies are the flowers of death.

EZRA: Did you bring any food?

DOROTHY: *(Trying to laugh it off.)* Ezra, really! Here I've come over three thousand miles to see you, and all you can think about is food!

EZRA: It's what you're good at, isn't it?

DOROTHY: As a matter of fact, you know perfectly well it was part of my contract that I'd never have to cook.

EZRA: So, what did you bring?

DOROTHY: Me.

EZRA: I can see that. What else?

DOROTHY: Nothing else. Flowers—and me. That's all.

OVERHOLSER: You must be tired, Mrs. Pound.

DOROTHY: Not one bit.

EZRA: You bring any word from "O"?

DOROTHY: "O" is Ezra's mistress. Olga Rudge, Doctor Overholser.

OVERHOLSER: Yes. *(Quietly.)* I realize.

DOROTHY: *(Smiles.)* Ezra's daughter, Mary, was born to Olga Rudge. Later on, I had Omar.

OVERHOLSER: Yes.

EZRA: He knows all that.

DOROTHY: I thought it might make it easier if Doctor Overholser heard it from me, Ezra. Miss Rudge and I get on very well, Doctor. Now.

EZRA: Liar. *(Pause.)* Well—did you bring me a letter? Anything?

DOROTHY: Nothing concrete, Ezra. *(Sotto voce to OVERHOLSER.)* I think he was hoping she'd send some money. *(Aloud, to EZRA.)* But she sends her love.

OVERHOLSER: Where are you staying in Washington, Mrs. Pound?

DOROTHY: For the moment, Mister Cornell has installed me in a small hotel. The Belvedere, I believe. But, of course, if Ezra is to be here longer, I shall find a room, perhaps a small apartment. It will depend on what money I can raise. *(Turns to EZRA.)* We are going to do everything in our power to get you out of here. You have so many friends, and they're all determined to set you free.

> *(She rummages in her purse.)*

OVERHOLSER: Mrs. Pound ...

DOROTHY: No, no, Doctor. Please. This will only take a moment. I want Ezra to see for himself how many friends he has ... here! *(She leafs through a pack of letters.)* Look, Ezra! Look! From Ernest Hemingway, from Marianne Moore, from Carl Sandburg, from Cal Lowell. Look, Ezra—look! From Archie MacLeish, from Mister Auden, from John dos Passos, Van Wyck Brooks, Tom Eliot ... Ezra! Ezra! Look!

> *(A spotlight reveals WILLIAMS watching the scene from a distance.)*

EZRA: Nothing there from Frost? Nothing from Bill Williams?

DOROTHY: Ezra, dear, all these people believe in you. All these giants ... want to help.

EZRA: But not Frost? Not Williams?

DOROTHY: Frost is coming round. He's difficult. And Bill ... you know Bill loves you, Ezra. He's been here to see you. He just hasn't written yet. But he will. I'm sure he will. *(Crosses to EZRA and embraces him.)* Please don't be sad. I've come to take care of you.

EZRA: *(Pushing her away.)* Don't do that. Don't hold onto me. Don't do that!

DOROTHY: *(Stepping back.)* All right, Ezra. I'm sorry.

EZRA: Give me those letters. *(He takes them.)*

DOROTHY: I'll have to have them back, of course. I have to reply to all of them.

EZRA: Did any money come with these?

DOROTHY: No.

EZRA: Then how are we going to live?

DOROTHY: The way we've always lived.

EZRA: I'm not being paid, any more, for my broadcasts, you know. There's no income there.

DOROTHY: I have some money in England, Ezra. You have some money from royalties. It just takes time to free it up. We'll be all right. *(Turns to OVERHOLSER.)* Could we step outside, Doctor? I'd like very much to see the rest of the hospital ...

OVERHOLSER: Of course.

EZRA: You going out there to talk about me?

DOROTHY: I want to see what this place is like, Ezra. That's all.

> *(OVERHOLSER moves towards DOROTHY, who pats EZRA on the arm.)*

OVERHOLSER: We won't be long, Mister Pound.

> *(OVERHOLSER escorts DOROTHY towards the movable table.)*

EZRA: *(Calling after them.)* Don't forget, Doctor. I want a woman.

> *(He sits down on his cot to look at the letters. The spotlight on WILLIAMS fades to black.)*

Scene Seven

> *(St. Elizabeth's corridor. Lights dim on EZRA's area, and come up on the movable table.)*

DOROTHY: Oh, my ...

OVERHOLSER: Are you all right, Mrs. Pound?

DOROTHY: Oh, yes. It's just the shock. To see him, you know. I've waited for this moment since October. I thought I was never going to get out of Italy. I've been so afraid. And not a word from Ezra. The only letters I had were from Mister Cornell, and I had begun to think he was hiding the truth from me. Was he, Doctor? What is the truth? Will Ezra ... hang? Be killed?

OVERHOLSER: I don't think you have to worry, Mrs. Pound.

DOROTHY: But they're hanging William Joyce. Lord Haw-Haw. And Ezra seems so hated—by the people—in the press. The press is terrible, here.

OVERHOLSER: Are you aware of what we mean to do? I mean about your husband?

DOROTHY: Mister Cornell says he's entered a plea of insanity.

OVERHOLSER: That's right.

DOROTHY: But Ezra Pound is not insane, Doctor Overholser. How can they say so?

OVERHOLSER: I think he is insane, Mrs. Pound.

DOROTHY: But ...

OVERHOLSER: Not in the actual sense, insane—only in the technical sense.

DOROTHY: *(Bitter, angry.)* There's a difference?

OVERHOLSER: There can be—if there needs to be.

DOROTHY: *(Sounding the words.)* There can be if there needs to be ... if there needs to be, there can be? I hope you aren't going to try to convince me with jargon, Doctor. I cannot cope with jargon. I've spent the last thirty years with Ezra Pound, trying to get him to talk to me in simple English. Tell me what you mean in a language I can understand.

OVERHOLSER: I mean that your husband is insane because I say so, and I'm his doctor.

DOROTHY: *(Sounding the words.)* Insane because you say so ...

OVERHOLSER: That's right.

DOROTHY: But how can I let you say that?

OVERHOLSER: You can think of William Joyce, Mrs. Pound. You can think of William Joyce and make your choice.

> *(DOROTHY sits on platform down right of the table. After a pause, she starts to laugh.)*

Mrs. Pound?

DOROTHY: *(Still laughing.)* Forgive me, Doctor. I'm sorry ... *(Winds down.)* It's just ... *(Laughs again.)*

OVERHOLSER: Mrs. Pound. Please.

DOROTHY: It rhymes, Doctor. *(Standing.)* It rhymes! That's all. "You can think of William Joyce and make your choice!" It rhymes.

> *(Still laughing, DOROTHY waves him off, making her way up the steps down left. She exits in the direction of the Public Gallery.)*

Scene Eight

(Courtroom, full light.)

CORNELL: *(Addressing the empty witness chair.)* Doctor Overholser …

OVERHOLSER: *(Still down right, looking in direction of DOROTHY's exit.)* Yes?

> *(During the following speech, OVERHOLSER becomes more aware of CORNELL, and moves slowly up to sit in the witness chair.)*

CORNELL: Based upon what you have indicated, how do you regard Ezra Pound's ability to answer questions in connection with the presentation of his defense, were he to be brought to trial in a criminal case?

OVERHOLSER: Well, with an infinite amount of patience and an infinite amount of time, it might be possible to get from Mister Pound a lucid answer to a question.

> *(During the rest of this scene, EZRA makes it clear that a developing headache is interrupting the reading of his letters.)*

CORNELL: In other words, would his discursiveness and inability to answer questions prevent his attorney from presenting his side of the picture in defense of this indictment?

OVERHOLSER: Yes. It would.

CORNELL: Thank you, Doctor. *(To MATLACK.)* Your witness.

> *(CORNELL returns to his place as MATLACK rises, papers in hand.)*

JUDGE: Mister Matlack?

MATLACK: *(Approaching the witness chair.)* Thank you, Your Honor. Doctor Overholser …

> *(OVERHOLSER seems lost in a reverie.)*

Doctor Overholser …

OVERHOLSER: Yes?

MATLACK: *(Consulting his papers.)* Would you characterize your definition of infinite as infinite … or as less than infinite?

OVERHOLSER: *(Surprised.)* As being infinite, Counsellor.

MATLACK: In other words … without end.

OVERHOLSER: Yes, sir.

MATLACK: Then, would you tell me, Doctor, what you meant when you said, "with an infinite amount of patience"—with an infinite amount of time, it might be possible get from Mister Pound a lucid answer to a question?

OVERHOLSER: I ...

MATLACK: Did you mean what you seemed to say, namely, that one day, a lucid answer might be forthcoming, depending on your patience and your time, or—

OVERHOLSER: Yes.

MATLACK: Doctor Overholser, I have not yet completed the question.

OVERHOLSER: I'm sorry.

MATLACK: Or did you mean, as you have just indicated through your definition of the word infinite, that lucid answers would never be forthcoming? And let me make clear, Doctor. As a result of what you say next, Ezra Pound will either spend the rest of his life in an insane asylum—or he will hang.

Scene Nine

(Holding room, St. Elizabeth's. All lights go out except for those that backlight the Court. A pounding is heard, along with the sound of a woman screaming. The lights come up in area of the movable table, to reveal a FEMALE PATIENT pounding on the table top. Two ORDERLIES run in from down right and stop before they reach her.)

FEMALE PATIENT: *(Pounding the table top.)* Kill! Kill! Kill! Kill! Kill!

(She continues this until the scene ends; she is EZRA's headache.)

ORDERLY ONE: *(Calling back to stage right.)* Get Doctor Stevens—!

ORDERLY TWO: I need assistance with the patient in 22!

ORDERLY ONE: You go on, I'll get Stevens.

(He runs off right while ORDERLY TWO hurries to the FEMALE PATIENT. Just as he reaches her, the lights on her area go out, and there is silence except for a distant, echoed pounding, which continues under the beginning of the next scene. After a moment, lights come up on EZRA, still seated on his cot, and on OVERHOLSER, still seated in the witness chair. MATLACK, during the melee, has withdrawn to his own table.)

Scene Ten

(EZRA's room, St. Elizabeth's.)

EZRA: *(Quietly.)* That woman down the hall wants my death.

OVERHOLSER: *(In the witness chair.)* Oh, I think not, Mister Pound. How have you been doing here today?

EZRA: *(Rising.)* I can't get comfortable.

OVERHOLSER: Are you sore anywhere? Physically sore?

> *(EZRA moves up and sits on the platform steps near OVERHOLSER.)*

EZRA: No. No. Except in my mind, of course. I always wondered why it was that people speak of headaches. I've never had a headache in my life, but I have had mind-aches.

OVERHOLSER: Yes.

EZRA: And I have one now that I think will drive me mad ... unless ...

> *(During the following, the distant pounding fades, but is still audible, along with the occasional sound of distant female weeping.)*

OVERHOLSER: *(Carefully.)* Mister Pound, I've been reading some of your work. *(Sincerely.)* I'm very admiring—very. I feel so privileged to be your doctor—grateful I was chosen for this ...

EZRA: *(Without grandeur.)* Your servant.

OVERHOLSER: *(Taking a small book from his jacket pocket.)* You are—you have written some of the greatest poetry I've ever encountered. That's the sum of it. It's difficult to say such things.

EZRA: Mebbe, but it ain't difficult to hear them, Doctor.

> *(They both laugh lightly.)*

What have you got there?

OVERHOLSER: The Mauberley poems. I read them last night, and again this morning.

EZRA: Let me see them.

> *(OVERHOLSER hands the book to EZRA, who leafs through it and stops at one page.)*

These fought in any case ... Oh, yes ... the war ...

> *(He is deeply moved, having forgotten the emotion of the poem. He reads:)*

There died a myriad,
And of the best, among them,
For an old bitch—gone in the teeth,
For a botched civilization ...

(Offstage, the FEMALE PATIENT continues weeping.)

Charm, smiling at the good mouth,
Quick eyes gone under earth's lid,
For two gross of broken statues,
For a few thousand battered ...

OVERHOLSER: ... books.

(The weeping and the pounding fade to silence. EZRA closes the book and sits for a moment, silent.)

EZRA: Must I spend the rest of my life in an asylum, Doctor?

OVERHOLSER: If you want to live, we must face that possibility.

EZRA: If I want to live. *(Pause.)* Do I want to live, Doctor?

OVERHOLSER: How can I possibly tell you that?

EZRA: No, no. Tell me. Tell me. You must. Tell me: do I want to live?

OVERHOLSER: *(Pause.)* Yes. *(Pause.)* Which is why you must not go to trial.

Scene Eleven

(Courtroom, full light. MATLACK is moving towards the witness chair. EZRA remains seated on steps.)

MATLACK: Doctor ...

OVERHOLSER: I ...

MATLACK: So what is your answer?

OVERHOLSER: What is the question?

MATLACK: Can we expect—at any time, ever—lucid answers from the defendant regarding the circumstances of his current condition.

(EZRA rises and starts to move towards his court chair.)

OVERHOLSER: I cannot answer that question. I've already said so.

EZRA: *(He stops near the chair.)* I can answer that question.

CORNELL: *(Rising, addressing EZRA.)* No!

EZRA: Let me answer it!

JUDGE: *(Bangs the gavel and addresses EZRA.)* Mister Pound. Clearly you do not understand your position in this courtroom. If you speak once more, you will be forced to take the stand. Do you understand that, sir?

EZRA: *(Taking a step towards the JUDGE.)* But I want to take the stand.

JUDGE: No you do not, sir. No, you do not!

CORNELL: *(Approaching EZRA, putting a hand on his arm.)* Mister Pound …

EZRA: Take your hands off me. I want to speak!

JUDGE: Mister Pound, sit down!

> *(The JUDGE bangs the gavel repeatedly through the following:)*

CORNELL: Mister Pound … Your Honor—Your Honor, I request the assistance of the Bailiff …

EZRA: You sick the fucking Bailiff on me, Cornell, I'll bite your head off!

JUDGE: *(Gavel.)* Bailiff! Bailiff! Remove Mister Pound from the Court!

> *(BAILIFF enters from right, and struggles EZRA off right.)*

I am calling noon recess. *(Single gavel.)* Court will reconvene in one hour and one half. *(Rises.)*

CLERK: All rise.

> *(The Court slowly empties, and lights dim except for stage left and down stage area.)*

Scene Twelve

> *(Courthouse corridor. WILLIAMS appears from direction of the Public Gallery, comes down the steps and starts across down stage area towards the right. DEUTSCH appears behind him and calls out as he approaches.)*

DEUTSCH: Doctor Williams … just a moment, please … *(He reaches WILLIAMS, who has stopped.)* Well, that was certainly unexpected!

WILLIAMS: Do you think so, Mister Deutsch? I've been waiting for it all morning.

DEUTSCH: Do you think this will do him some damage?

WILLIAMS: You sound as though you rather hope it will, Mister Deutsch.

> *(During the following, they make their way across the front of the stage towards the right.)*

DEUTSCH: Well, he's guilty, that's for sure. And I'd hate to see him get off just because they say he's insane.

WILLIAMS: Would you like to see him hang, in that case?

DEUTSCH: He should be made to pay somehow.

WILLIAMS: Perhaps life imprisonment would satisfy you.

DEUTSCH: *(Angry.)* Doctor Williams, are you a Jew?

WILLIAMS: *(Stops.)* I beg your pardon?

DEUTSCH: Are you a Jew?

WILLIAMS: No, sir. I am not.

DEUTSCH: I am.

WILLIAMS: Oh. I see. Then you have my sympathy.

DEUTSCH: I what? *(Laughs bitterly.)* I have your what?

WILLIAMS: My sympathy, Mister Deutsch. I mean because of Ezra's diatribes—his attacks on your religion and your people.

DEUTSCH: *(Calming.)* Well, then …

WILLIAMS: Will you take lunch with me, Mister Deutsch?

DEUTSCH: Yes, sir. Yes. I will.

> *(They begin to move again towards the right exit, but WILLIAMS stops.)*

WILLIAMS: Old Ez has always spoken ill of your race, Mister Deutsch. It's there in his work, it's there in his letters, there in his conversations. Always has been. But that, of course, is not why he's on trial.

DEUTSCH: It should be.

WILLIAMS: No. No. We cannot put people on trial because of their opinions. That is not why we are here. Shall we proceed, Mr. Deutsch?

> *(They exit right.)*

Scene Thirteen

> *(Courtroom. Partial light, except where MATLACK sits at his table eating a sandwich. Otherwise, the room is empty. ANDERSON enters from the left.)*

ANDERSON: Isaiah?

MATLACK: *(Mouth full.)* Uhmmm?

ANDERSON: There's someone here you should see …

MATLACK: Can it wait?

ANDERSON: It's one of the doctors from St. Elizabeth's.

MATLACK: Oh?

ANDERSON: Yes. A Doctor Carlos Dalmau.

MATLACK: *(Interest piqued.)* Unh-hunh?

ANDERSON: I think you might want to see him.

MATLACK: Okay. Bring him in.

> *(As ANDERSON exits left, MATLACK screws up the wax paper from his lunch and throws it into a waste basket under the table. ANDERSON reappears with DALMAU. MATLACK rises, offering his hand.)*

Doctor Dalmau? I'm Isaiah Matlack.

DALMAU: *(Nervous, accepting his hand.)* Counsellor ...

MATLACK: *(Sitting.)* Please sit down. I was just finishing my lunch. I don't like to leave the Courthouse on days like this. Too distracting, especially when your cross-examination is interrupted ... *(Laughs lightly.)*

ANDERSON: I think what Doctor Dalmau has to say is important, Isaiah.

MATLACK: What is it, then? Something about Ezra Pound?

DALMAU: *(Sitting.)* No. Not Pound. Overholser.

MATLACK: Overholser?

DALMAU: Yes.

MATLACK: *(To ANDERSON.)* Keep a watch, Don. If anyone comes, I'm not available.

ANDERSON: *(Walks a few steps, his back to the others.)* Okay. Just remember, we have very little time.

MATLACK: All right, Doctor Dalmau. Shoot.

DALMAU: To begin with, Doctor Overholser is a man I admire. I mean, in my profession, the profession of psychiatry. This is not about professional jealousy, in other words. I want to make that clear.

MATLACK: *(Smiling.)* No knives, you mean. Okay.

DALMAU: Mister Matlack, were you aware that when Mister Pound was incarcerated in Italy, at Pisa, in the American Detention Centre there, he was examined by three American psychiatrists?

MATLACK: No. I wasn't aware of that.

DALMAU: Army psychiatrists.

MATLACK: I see.

DALMAU: Well, Doctor Overholser knew about these examinations—and also, the outcome—the conclusion drawn by those doctors over there.

MATLACK: Which was?

DALMAU: Which was that Ezra Pound is sane.

MATLACK: All three of them said that—came to that conclusion?

DALMAU: Yes, sir.

MATLACK: I see. *(To ANDERSON.)* Donald, get out of here. Telephone the Justice Department and see if we have any record of these examinations. Surely, if they exist, they would have come to us. Though God knows why we haven't heard of them till this.

   (ANDERSON starts away. MATLACK stops him.)

And if we don't have them, find out what you can from the Army. Someone must have kept such records. Ask if there's any possibility they're still in Italy.

ANDERSON: Done. *(Exits left.)*

MATLACK: *(Pause.)* All three, eh? Every one of 'em: sane.

DALMAU: That's right, sane. And there's more.

MATLACK: Good heavens. What?

DALMAU: Did Doctor Overholser tell you in Court this morning the conclusions drawn by other psychiatrists on the staff at St. Elizabeth's, after they had examined Mister Pound?

MATLACK: No. He didn't.

DALMAU: Well, I happen to know that Doctor Overholser will have the results of these other psychiatrists' individual examinations with him on the stand this afternoon. Get him to read them.

MATLACK: Why?

DALMAU: Because not all the doctors at St. Elizabeth's agree with Doctor Overholser's official diagnosis that Ezra Pound is insane. Several, in fact, disagree quite vehemently. You should ask Doctor Overholser especially for the conclusions of Drs. Stevens, Waldrop, Keeney and Duval. And myself, of course.

MATLACK: *(Writing.)* Stevens, Waldrop, Keeney, and Duval ...

DALMAU: And Dalmau. Carlos Dalmau. D-a-l-m-a-u.

(Lights fade on MATLACK and DALMAU.)

Scene Fourteen

(EZRA's room at St. Elizabeth's. Lights come up simultaneously on Ezra's centre stage area and down stage right, where an ORDERLY enters, escorting EZRA to his room. They are followed by DOROTHY and MARTINELLI, who carries a sketching pad. EZRA sits on his cot.)

DOROTHY: You can go on with your drawing, Miss Martinelli, and perhaps we can persuade Ezra to read to us. You're getting quite a good likeness of him, you know.

MARTINELLI: *(Delighted.)* Oh? You think so, Mrs. Pound? He has such a wonderful head.

(EZRA picks up some pages and thrusts one at MARTINELLI.)

EZRA: Here. Read this.

(MARTINELLI, enraptured, sets the sketching pad on the stool, takes the page and silently reads.)

Out loud! Read it out loud!

MARTINELLI: *(Even more enraptured, launches into EZRA's new poem.)* Love, then was lightning enduring 5,000 years ...

EZRA: *(Without rancour.)* No. Not right. Give it back.

MARTINELLI: I'd much rather hear you read your poems, anyway. I could listen to your voice all day.

(EZRA looks at her for a moment, then busies himself with a pencil. DOROTHY walks over, picks up the sketching pad and hands it to MARTINELLI.)

DOROTHY: You should have seen Ezra when he was young, Miss Martinelli. His hair was the colour of flames. I swear, when I saw him first, I thought he'd been set on fire! This great, tall man with blazing hair and green eyes. Oh! He was wonderful, then.

MARTINELLI: It must be awfully hard, just to let it go—the past.

DOROTHY: Yes and no. It's gone, of course. But parts of it endure—the images, remembered feelings ...

EZRA: *(Reading triumphantly.)* There it is! Love, gone as lightning, enduring 5,000 years.

MARTINELLI: How beautiful!

DOROTHY: Yes.

EZRA: *(Setting the pages aside.)* Did you say your name was Cheri?

MARTINELLI: No. It's Sheri.

EZRA: *(He thinks it's ugly.)* Sheri ... Oh.

DOROTHY: Sheri Martinelli.

EZRA: I prefer Cheri.

MARTINELLI: Then Cheri it is!

EZRA: Only if you learn to pronounce it.

MARTINELLI: Cheri? Cheri? Cherry?

> *(EZRA and MARTINELLI laugh. DOROTHY smiles.)*

DOROTHY: You see, Miss Martinelli, I told you you would get along. *(Pause.)* I think I'll just go and see if one of the nurses can direct me to a wool shop. I ... have some knitting I'd like to finish. *(She starts to leave.)* I may be a while. I'm hungry, so when I get back I think what I'll do is go on down to the cafeteria and get myself a sandwich.

EZRA: *(Staring at MARTINELLI.)* Take your time.

MARTINELLI: Yes.

DOROTHY: Goodbye, then.

MARTINELLI: *(Remembering to be polite.)* Goodbye, Mrs. Pound.

> *(As the lights fade on EZRA and MARTINELLI, DOROTHY pauses and looks back.)*

DOROTHY: *(Smiling.)* Done. *(She exits.)*

Scene Fifteen

> *(An Italian restaurant. Lights come up on the movable table. WILLIAMS and DEUTSCH are seated, each with a wine glass. There is also a wine bottle.)*

WILLIAMS: *(Pouring wine for both.)* All through the war, I missed the wines of Europe. One of the benefits Ezra had by staying there. *(Drinks reflectively.)* You know, it's easy to forget he made his choices. Europe wasn't foisted on him ...

DEUTSCH: No.

(During the rest of this scene, MARTINELLI exits and the members of the COURT casually take their places in the dimly lit, backlit courtroom. On the scrim is a rear-projection of falling snow. Light slowly picks out EZRA, seated on his cot. An offstage piano plays "Banks of the Wabash.")

WILLIAMS: Choices ... choices ... *(Pause.)* You know, watching him there in Court this morning—hearing them talk about what he's said and what he's done—the intellectual horror of the broadcasts, the appalling errors in judgment ... Ezra always thinks he's being terribly profound when, in fact, he hasn't the least idea of when he hits true and when he falls flat. He wants, above all else, to be praised, Mister Deutsch. He's got to be loved, to be praised, and so, in spite of everything, one loves and one praises him.

DEUTSCH: In other words, you do his bidding.

WILLIAMS: No, no, no. I love the man, Mister Deutsch, as one might love an idiot ... I love him for his sweet character. And I mourn the fact that, of that sweet character, not one jot or tittle has made an appearance in that courtroom. This is sad, Mister Deutsch. For me, a great sadness.

Scene Sixteen

(Courtroom. As the music continues, the rear-projection of snow fades and the light slowly rises on the Court. DEUTSCH and WILLIAMS exit left with their glasses and bottle. EZRA rises and walks over to sit, for the first time, in his court chair. When the lights are fully up, and the music finished, the trial resumes, with OVERHOLSER in the witness chair, and MATLACK near him.)

MATLACK: Doctor Overholser, I believe you said this morning that your opinion of Ezra Pound's condition was based in part on your own observations, and partly on your examinations of the records.

OVERHOLSER: That is right.

MATLACK: Do you have those records with you?

OVERHOLSER: Yes, I do. They're in my brief case. But I can summarize ...

MATLACK: May we have them here? Your Honor?

JUDGE: The Clerk will get them.

(CLERK walks to CORNELL's table, picks up the brief case and delivers it to OVERHOLSER before returning to his place.)

MATLACK: Have you, yourself, been treating Mister Pound or has that been left to your associates at St. Elizabeth's?

OVERHOLSER: Partly to my associates.

MATLACK: *(Indicates briefcase.)* Are the records in your possession the records of those associates?

OVERHOLSER: Yes, they are.

MATLACK: Would you, when you can—take your time—refer to what those records show and thereby indicate the current state of Ezra Pound's mental health?

OVERHOLSER: *(Laughs, accepts brief case from CLERK, opens it and takes out a fat file.)* Well, as you will see—ah, yes, here we are—this is a rather bulky document.

MATLACK: Yes, I can see that. But I think we can do this quite economically, Doctor. Would you please turn to the entry of Doctor Harold Stevens?

OVERHOLSER: *(He is floored.)* Uhhh … yes. *(He leafs through pages.)* Doctor Stevens?

MATLACK: Yes. Doctor Harold Stevens.

OVERHOLSER: Right. Yes. I've found it. *(Playing for time.)* It's fairly lengthy …

MATLACK: Would you read Doctor Stevens' summation, please? That should be brief.

OVERHOLSER: His summation? Yes. *(He turns more pages.)* Summation: *(Coughs.)* I find …

MATLACK: Louder, please.

OVERHOLSER: *(Reluctantly louder.)* I find no abnormal mental condition is elicitable. H. Stevens, MD.

MATLACK: *(Refers to his notes.)* And the summation of Doctor Daniel Keeney, please?

OVERHOLSER: Keeney, Keeney … *(Leafing through more pages.)* No abnormal content was elicited. D. Keeney, MD.

MATLACK: And Doctor Neil Waldrop?

OVERHOLSER: *(Turns more pages.)* Unable to elicit any psychotic content at this time. N. Waldrop, MD.

MATLACK: Thank you. Just one more, Doctor. Would you read the summation of Doctor Bernard Duval, please?

OVERHOLSER: Duval?

MATLACK: Yes. Bernard Duval. Please.

OVERHOLSER: *(Turns more pages.)* No psychotic ideation was mani-
fested. *(Coughs.)* Bernard Duval, MD.

MATLACK: Thank you, Doctor Overholser. Now, Doctor, I'm going to
interrupt your testimony for just one moment, in order ... *(Crosses to
be closer to the JUDGE.)* Your Honor, I would like to enlist the
assistance of the Court Recorder.

JUDGE: Very well, she is at your disposal. But I hope you will make this
brief.

MATLACK: Yes, sir. *(To RECORDER.)* Miss Adams, would you repeat
some testimony for me, please. Doctor Overholser's responses to the
Defense Attorney, before the lunch recess?

RECORDER: Yes, sir.

MATLACK: Would you locate Doctor Overholser's answers—the part
about the defendant's transfer to St. Elizabeth's.

RECORDER: *(At her machine.)* Yes, sir. *(Pause. She looks for the right
place and reads.)* Witness: He was admitted to St. Elizabeth's on
January 1st and has been there ever since, somewhat more than one
month.

MATLACK: Would you continue reading, please? I will tell you when
to stop.

RECORDER: Yes sir. *(She reads.)* Counsel: Has he been under constant
observation? Witness: Yes. I spent a long time in consultation with
him just last Thursday, in fact. Counsel: But others, as well, other
doctors besides yourself have been observing him? Witness: Yes. I
have before me the report made by other physicians at the hospital,
and reading it, I see no reason to change my opinion.

MATLACK: Thank you, Miss Adams. *(Returns to his place beside the
witness chair.)* I have before me the report of the other physicians at
the hospital and, reading it, I see no reason to change my opinion.
(Pause.) Doctor Overholser?

　(OVERHOLSER stares at him in silence.)

Well, Doctor, you have read to us, just a moment ago, the conclusions
of four of those doctors—not one of whom agreed with your diagnosis of Mister Pound's mental condition. Not one. And yet, you said
this morning that, on the basis of these doctors' findings, you felt no
need to change your opinion.

OVERHOLSER: I ...

MATLACK: Have I missed something here? Are there, perhaps, twenty other opinions recorded in that report which do agree with your diagnosis?

OVERHOLSER: No, sir.

MATLACK: Are there any others?

OVERHOLSER: Yes, sir. One.

MATLACK: And whose opinion is that?

OVERHOLSER: Doctor Dalmau.

MATLACK: Would that be Doctor Carlos Dalmau?

OVERHOLSER: Yes.

MATLACK: And his opinion? Just the summation.

OVERHOLSER: *(He turns a page and clears his throat.)* Uhmmm ... Though the patient is clearly eccentric and suffering from depression, I could find no evidence of a psychotic condition. Carlos Dalmau, MD.

MATLACK: *(Pause.)* Doctor Overholser. On the basis of what we have just heard, I am forced to ask you, sir, just who in the name of hell do you think you are!

CORNELL: Objection!

MATLACK: *(Riding right through.)* Just who in the name of hell do you think you are, sir? Five doctors, five opinions—five, count them, five: Doctor Stevens, Keeney, Waldrop, Duval, Dalmau! Every single one of them could find no traces of insanity in the defendant. And yet you overruled them with your single opinion that Ezra Pound is crazy.

OVERHOLSER: Insane. We never call insane persons crazy.

MATLACK: Well, I'll tell you what, sir. I am more than inclined to call you crazy!

CORNELL: *(Rising.)* Objection.

JUDGE: Mister Matlack! *(Bangs gavel.)* You know the rules. Apply them.

MATLACK: *(Coming down against his will.)* Yes, sir. Yes. I withdraw my last remark. *(Pause.)* All right. *(Beat.)* All right. *(Drinks water.)* Now, Doctor Overholser, I understand that what we are concerned with in this inquiry into Ezra Pound's mental state is not a question of the difference between right and wrong—that is, Mister Pound's ability to distinguish between right and wrong—but rather, whether he is able to consult with Counsel and conduct a defense.

OVERHOLSER: That is correct.

MATLACK: Did he give you, in his general history, anything about his belief in Fascism?

OVERHOLSER: I did not discuss that with him particularly.

EZRA: *(Rising, knocking his chair over in doing so, shouting.)* I never did believe in Fascism! Goddamn it, I am opposed to Fascism!

(General reaction from the Court.)

JUDGE: *(Bangs the gavel repeatedly.)* Order, please. Order!

(General reaction subsides. CORNELL rights EZRA's chair, seats him back in it.)

MATLACK: Doctor Overholser, I don't know whether you've answered the question or not.

JUDGE: I think Mister Pound has answered it for him.

MATLACK: Did Ezra Pound ever discuss his advocacy of Mussolini, Doctor, and of Mussolini's politics?

OVERHOLSER: In the most general terms. Yes. But I didn't go into that in great detail, either. I looked upon that as a political matter.

MATLACK: Well, that's precisely what I'm getting at, Doctor. The politics. Did you ever read the defendant's book entitled Jefferson and Mussolini?

OVERHOLSER: No.

MATLACK: Did you take into consideration the fact that, living in Italy, where the political philosophy was Fascism, that Ezra Pound may have become imbued with that philosophy?

CORNELL: *(Rising.)* Your Honor, I object to this line of questioning and characterization of Mister Pound. It is very distressing for him.

MATLACK: *(Almost losing control.)* It should be distressing for him! Because, when he stands trial for treason, it will be the answers to these questions, and this characterization, he will have to defend!

CORNELL: Your Honor, I object again! Counsel has used the word "when" in describing …

JUDGE: Mister Cornell, I have not yet ruled on your first objection.

When I have done so, I will entertain your second. One objection at a time, please.

CORNELL: Yes, Your Honor. But …

JUDGE: Be still, Mister Cornell. Be quiet. *(Pause.)* Now, Mister Matlack, I understand what you are attempting to achieve here and I will give you a certain latitude. But you must try not to disturb Mister Pound, if you can help it.

MATLACK: Yes, Your Honor. Thank you.

JUDGE: Mister Cornell, you had a second objection, I believe.

CORNELL: Yes, sir. Counsel has used the word "when" in describing the outcome of this hearing, and I quote, "when he stands trial for treason." We do not yet know whether any such trial will take place. Counsel should be instructed to say, "if" he stands trial for treason, not "when."

JUDGE: Sustained. Mister Matlack, you will refrain from using the word "when" inappropriately. Please continue …

MATLACK: Doctor Overholser, did Ezra Pound reveal to you, in the course of your examinations, that he had already been given a psychiatric examination in Italy?

OVERHOLSER: *(Shaken. He lies.)* No, sir. Where, in Italy?

MATLACK: At Pisa, in the Detention Centre. *(Checks papers.)* In fact, he was examined there not by one but three Unites States Army psychiatrists. Did he not tell you that?

OVERHOLSER: *(Lying.)* No.

   (General muttering in the Court.)

MATLACK: And you have been unaware of these examinations at Pisa until now? Until I mentioned them just now?

OVERHOLSER: *(A lie.)* Yes.

MATLACK: You were unaware of them.

OVERHOLSER: Yes.

MATLACK: And, therefore, unaware of the summations of these three separate psychiatric examinations?

OVERHOLSER: Yes.

JUDGE: What were the verdicts in Italy, Mister Matlack? You are trying my patience with this.

MATLACK: The summations, Your Honor, or the verdicts, as you call them, were unanimous.

JUDGE: And?

MATLACK: They found that Ezra Pound was sane—and perfectly capable of standing trial.

(General uproar in the Court.)

JUDGE: *(Banging his gavel repeatedly.)* Order! Order! Order! Order! Order!

EZRA: *(Rising.) I will speak!!!*

Scene Seventeen

(On EZRA's words, the lights on the Court dim slightly, and all motion ceases. EZRA rises from his chair and takes over centre stage, where he will wander during the following, in brighter light. As he begins, DOROTHY, MARTINELLI, WILLIAMS and BEATTY and the ORDERLY/REPORTERS enter separately at different times from different points, and stand listening.)

EZRA: I am ... I am ... I am here, now. And tempus loquendi, tempus tacendi. There is a time for speaking and a time to be silent. And ... the time to be silent is past. Gone, now. Departed. Over. I have not enjoyed the silence. My silence. And I have not enjoyed the spectacle, here, of my portrait. I have not lived my life—I have not been myself, for wages. I have never been myself—I have been Ezra Pound on account—I have always been paid in kind. A word for a word, a thought for a thought, a gesture for a gesture. And if I was silent, then all the others owed me a silence in return! But they have paid me out of an account I never garnered or deserved. To be called mad— madman—to be called insane, when I am not insane but only Ezra Pound. *I am Ezra Pound! I am Ezra Pound! (His voice catches.)* I came down into the valley from the mountain. I came down carrying books. I came down, thinking: they are here, now, and I must go to them and offer them my services. Mine, you see, my services were unique. And I said: it is I.

(Offstage a piano plays "Banks of the Wabash.")

There was a black man there in uniform. A Negro, very large, yet kind and gentle. And he called me the old man. There's an old man here who wants to help, he said to the others. And to me, he said: We'll take you in and see what you can do. And I was driven then, in the back of a truck, and they took me—somewhere—I don't remember— I cannot recall—but somewhere where everyone you saw was an American, everyone an American soldier. That's Ezra Pound, said one of them. We have been looking for Ezra Pound and there he is ...

(Pause. The sound of nails being hammered.)

Fascist! Traitor! Broadcasts! Treason!

(Hammering fades.)

I was not sending Axis propaganda, but my own. Doesn't anyone remember? Before every broadcast, there was a statement read. And the statement was: On the principle of free expression of opinion on the part of those qualified to have an opinion, Doctor Ezra Pound has been granted the freedom of the microphone twice a week ... I was never asked to say anything in those broadcasts. It was my own propaganda. Mine. I spoke out, not against my country, but against what my country was doing. Not against my country, but against the conspiracy in my country to bring my country down. Roosevelt, Morgenthau, Lehman, Baruch! Well, naturally, anyone who speaks out—who spoke against the Roosevelt-Morgenthau gang of Jews was a traitor! Well, so I said, so I said, so I said in my broadcasts: I will not submit to the whims and tactics of this gang—and I urged all my listeners to go and do likewise! I told them—I said: the first step towards a bright new world is to git onto Roosevelt and his works! An' the second step towards a bright new world is to *eliminate him and all his damned gang from public life in America! (Breathless.)* The alternative is ... the alternative is ... the alternative is the annihilation—the end of everything decent the United States of America ever stood for ... *(Pause. He continues subdued.)* That's all I did. That was all I did. I told—I told the truth. I pointed out—I just kept pointing out the truth. For which I now am called—am being called a crazy man—insane and crazy, mad, in this Court of law. This Court of Laws, which is not only here for justice, but for Justice Laws himself, who said, who says, I urge them to proceed upon the destruction of Ezra Pound ...

(There is an echoed sound of water dripping.)

Confucius is the only basis on which a world order can work. And I have returned to America to tell you so. The Chinese Empire, during its greatest periods, offers the only working model that can possibly serve in the present situation. We have come through a very large and devastating war and ... Confucius started as a Market Inspector and he rose to be Prime Minister and he gave more thought to the problem of vast administration than any simple highbrow philosopher. And I do not know if I would have arrived at the centre of his meaning if I had not been down underneath the collapse of a regime. Oh, god— goddamn! Benito and Clara—Mussolini and Petraci—strung up by the heels in a public square in Milan. *It should not have ended thus ...* And if I. If I ... And if I ...

> *(Sound of trucks wheeling into a courtyard, shots being fired, people crying out in fear and pain.)*

And if I had not been in the hands of friends—of friends—when I was driven, on my way to Pisa, into the courtyard of Chiavari, I would have been shot then and there, because ...

ORDERLY/REPORTERS: *Aiuto!!*

> *(Sound of shots.)*

EZRA: ... and they were shooting them, all the others who had been visible—and I had been visible—I had been heard. *Now, you want to do that for them!! To kill—kill—kill me!*

Scene Eighteen

> *(The lights alter slightly as the standing figures of others speak inside EZRA's mind, while EZRA fails to locate or see any of them.)*

DOROTHY: *(Very quiet.)* Ezra ...?

CORNELL: Mister Pound ...?

MARTINELLI: Maestro ...?

WILLIAMS: Ezra ... you poor dumb cluck!

EZRA: *(Lost.)* Bill?

WILLIAMS: Listen, instead of sounding off on your pathetic little ego-tooter, why don't you use what is left of your head and try to think a little while ...?

DOROTHY: Rest, Ezra. Rest, my darling ...

MARTINELLI: That was a beautiful poem. Every word was beautiful.

WILLIAMS: Maybe, since thinking is something that is probably not possible for you at the moment, why not just try for a few accurate statements? Start with simple things, like saying: Did I brush my teeth this morning?

BEATTY: *(Singing.)*
   Oh, the moonlight's fair
   Tonight along the Wabash ...

EZRA: I want you all to know that I came down the mountain and gave myself up.

DOROTHY: Are you cold? Are you feeling the cold? Here, let me give you this sweater which I have made for you. *(There is no sweater.)*

EZRA: There was a black man. A Negro. I turned myself in. I was not fleeing from justice.

BEATTY: Don't they ever turn the lights out around this place?

EZRA: You know—I have always thought I would outdo Dante Allegheri with my Cantos. Yes. But, you know, it is very difficult to write a Paradiso when all the indications are that you ought to write an apocalypse.

WILLIAMS: Ezra, I have to say this to you. It has to be said: No one forgives you for what you did. No one. You might as well realize, Ez, there is a point in all controversy beyond which a man's life, his last card, is necessarily forfeit. A man accepts that, Ez, and goes on—his eyes open. But when the showdown comes, he loses his life.

EZRA: So no one forgives me for what I did, eh? No one ...

WILLIAMS: That's right, Ezra. No one.

> *(WILLIAMS, MARTINELLI and the ORDERLY/REPORTERS fade to the edges of the stage; BEATTY moves to the movable table; DOROTHY to the centre stage stool and sits; DEUTSCH appears down left and stands, watching. The jury FOREMAN enters from right and is then still. EZRA slowly walks over and sits in his Court chair as the lights gradually rise to the usual level on the Court.)*

Scene Twenty

(Courtroom.)

JUDGE: *(Bangs gavel.)* Mister Pound, will you rise?

> *(As EZRA starts to rise, CORNELL moves down towards him.)*

CORNELL: Here, I'll help you.

EZRA: No. I can stand by myself.

CLERK: Mister Foreman, has the jury agreed upon its verdict?

FOREMAN: It has.

CLERK: What say you as to the respondent, Ezra Pound? Is he of sound or unsound mind?

FOREMAN: Unsound mind.

(General hubbub in the Court. EZRA sits in the Court chair.)

CLERK: Members of the Jury …

DOROTHY: Saved …

CLERK: … your Foreman says you find the respondent, Ezra Pound …

MARTINELLI: Thank heaven …

CLERK: … of unsound mind, and that is your verdict—so say you each and all?

(During the following, eleven of the people on the stage will say, "Yea.")

WILLIAMS: Well, Ez, there you are.

EZRA: Yes. Here I am. Declared insane—and unforgiven for what I have done.

WILLIAMS: Yes. But, Ezra, everyone forgives you for what you are, my old friend. Goodbye. *(He exits.)*

CLERK: All rise.

(The Court rises, JUDGE exits right, and the Court begins to empty.)

EZRA: Well …

CORNELL: Well, indeed. We won.

EZRA: You think?

CORNELL: I know.

EZRA: I'm not so sure.

DEUTSCH: *(Moves partly towards centre.)* You bastard, Pound. You got away with it. You got away with it. *(He turns and starts out down left, but stops and turns back.)* You bastard. *You goddamn bastard, Pound! (He exits down left.)*

Scene Twenty-one

(The stage now has only EZRA, DOROTHY and BEATTY on it. DOROTHY remains seated on the stool, BEATTY stands centre of the movable table and EZRA gets up during the following and

moves to sit on his cot. There is the sound of a rising wind in a hollow place.)

EZRA: Do not move. Let the wind speak. That is paradise. Let the gods forgive what I have made. Let those I love try to forgive what I have made.

DOROTHY: Can we go now, Ezra?

(Offstage a piano plays "Banks of the Wabash" from here to the end of the play.)

Please, can we go? I'm cold.

(She rises and goes partway to right.)

EZRA: To confess wrong without losing rightness. A little light, like a rush light. To lead back to splendour.

(DOROTHY exits right.)

BEATTY: *(Pause. Moving closer to EZRA.)* You been here long?

EZRA: All my life, it seems.

BEATTY: Tell me your name, old man.

EZRA: Pound. Ezra Pound. Custodian.

(Music and lights slowly fade. The End.)